Private Practice Psychology

Private Practice Psychology: A Handbook

Richard T. Kasperczyk
and
Ronald D. Francis

BPS BOOKS THE BRITISH PSYCHOLOGICAL SOCIETY

First published in 2001 by BPS Books (The British Psychological Society),
St Andrews House, 48 Princess Road East, Leicester, LE1 7DR, UK.

A catalogue record for this book is available from the British Library.

Library of Congress Cataloging-in-Publication Data on file.

ISBN 1 85433 343 7

Typeset by Book Production Services, London

Printed in Great Britain by MPG Books Limited, Bodmin, Cornwall

Distributed by Plymbridge Distributors, Estover, Plymouth, PL6 7PZ, UK.

Whilst every effort has been made to ensure the accuracy of the contents of this publication, the publishers and authors expressly disclaim responsibility in law for negligence or any cause of action whatsoever. This book is of an advisory, instructive, and resource nature. It is not intended to have any legal force, nor to supplant any professional advice that might apply. This work should always be seen as subordinate to legal considerations and professional advice. Neither the writers nor the publishers can be held responsible for its use in particular circumstances, and both disclaim responsibility for the book's use in places and circumstances far from their control. Where commercial organisations are mentioned it is done by way of illustration – not as an endorsement.

Contents

Acknowledgements

This book has its origins in an Australian publication entitled *The Manual of Private Practice Psychology*, published by Macmillan Australia in 1997. That work was written by the two present authors and seemed to fill a significant market niche. This present work was totally rewritten for the United Kingdom environment. It is hoped that it will be found of value to UK readers who might be contemplating private practice in a branch of psychology. As is mentioned in the text, whether or not reading this work results in a re-consideration of being a private practitioner or of going ahead with private practice, it will have fulfilled its purpose. If it results in practice improvement, that too will be a success.

It will be appreciated that a work such as this could not have been created at a distance. The second author was fortunate in having a congenial environment in Britain to do the necessary local work. A Visiting Fellowship at Clare Hall in Cambridge provided such a background. Sincere thanks are offered to Dame Gillian Beer, President of Clare Hall, and to the Fellows of Clare Hall. The universities in which the second author has positions (Monash University and Victoria University, both in Melbourne) have been models of helpfulness and encouragement.

The first author is also pleased to acknowledge the help and advice of several colleagues, and of the staff in his practice for their efficient and valuable help. Maaike Jacobs of BT also gave helpful advice.

Within the British Psychological Society, Joyce Collins, Rachel Gear, Andy Burman, and Russell Hobbs were – and are – what every author would like: courteous, competent and efficient. Derek Atkins, copy editor, has made valuable contributions. Two fellow psychologists, Dr Deborah Hunt and Bella Robinson-Bell, provided some valuable insights, as did Dr Gisli Gudjonsson. Heidi Dyson of Cambridge, expert in starting and developing small businesses, was particularly helpful. Professor Noel Sheehy of Queens University in Belfast provided particularly useful evaluations and suggestions for improvement, which have been incorporated. Sincere thanks go to Gloria-Lesly Francis for most valuable editorial advice.

Regrettably, such help leaves us with no one else to blame for any shortcomings in this work.

Richard Kasperczyk
Ronald Francis
October 2000

1

Introduction

1.1 About this book

Psychology has been identified as a fast-growing profession, with 30,000 students being enrolled in A-level Psychology. Growth of membership of the British Psychological Society is about 7 per cent per annum, with an anticipated membership of 50,000 by the year 2006. More graduates are expected to enter the market with a view to putting up their practice plate and earning their living by independent means. At the same time, no corresponding change has been observed in the training of psychologists to manage a professional practice. Support for the psychologist in private practice has not kept up with either demand or expectations.

This book aims – at least partly – to fill that void. Its ambition is to add to the profession of psychology by providing the practitioner with foundation skills in managing a practice. On the more practical and less altruistic side, the authors, along with quite a few other practitioners, expect to spend less time answering the questions from those starting out, as many of the answers are contained in this book.

1.2 The target reader

The book has been written with a wide readership in mind, ranging from students who contemplate working in private practice through to the very experienced practitioners who would like to either expand or sell their practices. The readers who are likely to benefit most, however, will be the psychologists who are serious about planning the establishment of their private practices. There is a small pamphlet published by the British Psychological Society entitled *Private Practice as a Psychologist* (1996). It is recommended that those proposing to enter private practice in psychology obtain a copy.

It will also be noted that other works have appeared on the subject of maintaining a private practice – but not for Britain. The available works are about legal and financial protection of a practice, or are confined to particular forms of practice such as mental health. This present work is essentially British, it is not restricted to particular forms of practice, and is not about legalistic and financial protection. It is about being creative rather than defensive, about psychology practice in the wider sense, and about the life of a practice from starting, through running and developing, to the sale at a later turning point in a practitioner's career.

1.3 Useful references

This handbook has been designed to guide both the prospective private practitioner and the present practitioner who wishes to improve or expand the practice. To this end, there are numerous other sources of information. These will include the British Psychological Society's *Professional Psychology Handbook* (1995) (of which, although now out of print, copies are still available in libraries), Francis and Cameron (1997), various website addresses available through any of the conventional search engines, the British Psychological Society pamphlets and guides, and various other bodies referred to in this text.

1.4 Defining private practice

'Private practice' and 'independent practice' will be used interchangeably throughout this book. They both mean the type of employment that involves generating income through independent means – that is, not through being employed by any organization. Private practice embraces those who practise on a part-time basis even if they obtain income from other jobs such as lecturing, and counselling in community centres or hospitals, on a salary or contract basis.

1.5 The 'road map' of this book

This book will take you through the whole journey of private practice, from thinking about starting it (Chapter 2), through to its development-planning and establishment (Chapters 3 and 4). By the end of Chapter 4, you are presumed to have a basic practice in operation. The next steps involve stretching you towards more businesslike approaches, pursuing excellence (Chapter 5), and strategies for expanding the practice. In that chapter you will find more elaborate marketing ideas.

The journey ends with selling the practice (in Chapter 6), which by now should be a thriving business worth much more than it was when you first began. It could be argued, from the business point of view, that what is contained in that chapter should be your aim throughout the development of your practice, so that you can reap the rewards of the long-term investment of time, effort, risk and energy that running a practice inevitably entails.

You might like to think of your practice as not only a source of satisfaction and income, but also as a form of superannuation when you reach retirement age. Some resource material can be found in the Appendices, as well as some useful samples of the documentation and other resources discussed in this handbook. Attention is also drawn to the useful, and well set out website of the British Psychological Society at <http://www.bps.org.uk>. The comprehensive index to this book is designed to help you find quick answers to frequently asked questions.

Before starting out in practice

2.1 The fundamentals

To be a reputable psychologist, a person must be formally recognized by professional membership. The UK government does not, at the time of writing, formalize registration to practise, although there is a vigorous movement to enact such a requirement. The term 'psychologist' is not a protected one: anyone may use it – but may not call themselves a Chartered Psychologist unless legally entitled to do so.

Readers might have noted the informative articles that have appeared in *The Psychologist* over the last several years on the issue of statutory registration. If and when that happens, the relevant Act of Parliament, and the regulations attached to it, will determine who is a psychologist. In the meantime, the British Psychological Society provides the most reputable form of recognition. Graduate membership of the Society is set out in its 1998 document *Criteria for Membership* and is supplemented by its 1999 *Conversion Qualifications*.

Membership of the British Psychological Society is open to a wide variety of psychologists. The route to Chartered status is through professional training. To be a specialist psychologist is usually to be a member of a specialist Division of the British Psychological Society (BPS); specialities are thus defined by the BPS Divisions that may exist at any one time. A Division is the route to Chartered status, and qualification results in the title Chartered (name of speciality) Psychologist (e.g., Chartered Occupational Psychologist).

The first stage of qualifying as a Chartered Psychologist (see the BPS 1999 pamphlet entitled *Chartered Psychologists*) is, in principle, by having one of the following:

- an accredited undergraduate degree (or an approved overseas degree);
- a recognized postgraduate qualification;

- a conversion course qualification;
- a Pass in the Society's qualifying examination.

This basic qualification equips the candidate to move on to the next stage. That is achieved by candidates needing to:

- have undergone approved postgraduate training and supervision;
- have been judged 'fit to practise' independently; and
- have agreed to follow the strict Code of Conduct and be answerable to a disciplinary system, in which non-psychologists form the majority.

More detailed information is available in the BPS booklet *Information on the Register of Chartered Psychologists* (1999). While membership of the BPS may be an advantage, it needs to be understood that it is not a legal prerequisite for psychology practice. Some of the advantages of membership are the recognized credibility and skills gained from ongoing professional development, an implicit commitment to the BPS Code of Conduct, and association with other professionals.

Within the British Psychological Society there are currently nine Divisions:

- Teachers and Researchers in Psychology;
- Clinical Psychology;
- Counselling Psychology;
- Forensic Psychology;
- Educational and Child Psychology;
- Scottish Division of Educational Psychology;
- Health Psychology;
- Occupational Psychology;
- Neuropsychology.

More detail is set out in the British Psychological Society's pamphlet *Information on the Divisions of the Society*. Further, there are sections and special groups within the Society. The sections currently in existence are:

- Cognitive Psychology;
- Consciousness and Experiential Psychology;
- Developmental Psychology;
- Education;
- History and Philosophy of Psychology;
- Lesbian and Gay Psychology;
- Mathematical, Statistical and Computing Psychology;
- Occupational Psychology;
- Psychobiology;

- Psychology of Women;
- Psychotherapy;
- Social Psychology;
- Sports and Exercise Psychology;
- Transpersonal Psychology.

Within the Society there is also currently a special group dealing with 'Psychologists and Social Services'.

It will be appreciated that the BPS Divisions are, amongst other things, the monitors of specialist qualifications and practice: the sections are composed of those psychologists with an interest in the designated areas. The common ground includes the maintenance of standards and the promotion of that particular area of psychology. Information on sections and special groups is available in a BPS pamphlet appropriately entitled *Information on the Sections and Special Groups of the Society*.

It is also assumed that, prior to starting out in private practice, not only is the professional practitioner qualified, accredited and registered, but also skilled and competent to practise. Psychology degrees do not necessarily equip the student with the applied skills for private practice. Conversely, psychology training does equip graduates with skills that are marketable in other contexts (e.g., numeracy, literacy, analytical thinking, and people management).

It can be argued that professional competence is more critical for private practitioners than for psychologists employed otherwise, simply because it is the clientele – the market – who make a judgement about the practitioner's competence every time they return and every time they pay their fees. The issues of professional development, peer networks, reviews and support, and accountability for the Code of Conduct, are essential ingredients in the life of a professional in private practice.

At the international level, it is noted that the European Federation of Professional Psychologists Associations (EFPPA) is moving towards creating a Europsychologists Diploma; see the EFPPA website for the latest information (Appendix B). That Federation is also useful for those whose ambit is Europe-wide psychology.

2.2 Taking stock

Any career transition or its commencement calls for some vocational introspection, but the move towards establishing your own private practice demands it. Consider the following points:

- What drives me towards becoming an independent income earner?
- What do I expect to gain from such a move that I cannot obtain from another job?

- What do I stand to lose from this venture – what are the risks?
- What are my skills, my strengths – and my weaknesses?
- What opportunities and threats does such a transition pose for me – and which factors outweigh the others?
- How will a change of this kind affect my life – and am I prepared for the consequences?

While this book is not meant to discourage you from choosing the private practice option, its message, very simply, is this: do not take this step lightly, for it is not as easy as it seems. There may be readers of this book who, as a result of reading and thinking about the issue, decide not to try private practice. In this sense the book will have achieved one of its goals. It is a sobering thought that many businesses fail within the first year, psychology businesses being no exception. If you are to succeed where many have failed, you must be prepared at least for the following:

- some start-up investment, although this does not need to be a lottery win;
- constant uncertainty of income;
- ongoing non-professional tasks, especially marketing and administration;
- professional isolation; and
- perpetual pressure on the availability of time.

Your position does not necessarily need to be a lonely or pressured one, particularly when you are well established and are possibly working in a team of professionals with support staff around you.

2.3 Your motivation

This part of the soul-searching exercise aims to help you decide whether private practice is for you and, if you are not sure, which of the possible alternatives to the solo practice is more suitable. Check whether your desire to enter private practice is motivated by:

- potential for greater income;
- more flexibility in your working conditions;
- the need for independence from others;
- the need to control your life;
- potential investment for retirement; or
- the desire for more challenge in your job.

If your motivation is financial, you will need patience because it may take a few years to get there. If, on the other hand, you identify with those whose first and foremost desire is independence and flexibility, you may relax because these are relatively easy to achieve. Your destiny, your workload and the level of your income are totally in your hands the moment you step out from a job that pays you a regular income.

2.4 Your expectations

Psychologists are trained largely by academics, who have a distinct view of the world. Lecturers operate on the academic model, which requires everything to be 'just so' (and that is as it should be in training). In practice, however, it is not a matter of trying to be perfect but rather of constant trying, occasionally making a less than sound judgement, but getting it mainly right – and continually improving.

As one businessman expressed it to the authors, 'business is a matter of juggling as many balls in the air as can usefully be done, while dropping the minimum number'. When juggling, particularly as a beginner, you will almost certainly drop a few balls. The trick is not to be upset by this fact, and not to think of it as failure. Even if you mainly succeed, you are still bound to lose some contracts, commissions, ideas, etc. Such losses are learning experiences and not to be considered as major setbacks. The overall success is what matters, not getting stunning results from every enterprise you undertake.

Psychologists committed to succeeding in their practice must also be prepared to spend much unpaid time playing multifaceted roles in establishing their practices. An alternative would be to expect to invest a substantial amount of money up front to purchase the services of others specializing in business planning, marketing, administration, accounting, information systems, customer service, etc, before your practice is able to afford these. If you are in a position to afford this assistance, the path to financial success is likely to be easier and the end can be achieved more promptly.

In our experience, most psychologists choose to invest their time in lieu of money, so as to reduce their financial risks, particularly when cash is only available through high-interest loans. It must be remembered that expending time on any work-related project or business development is just as valid an investment as a financial one. It can bring much reward, and such time should be properly costed into the overall equation of business development.

For example, it may be helpful to charge out your time to an imaginary client at a reasonable hourly rate that is equivalent to the lost earnings opportunity from spending time on developing the business, so that the true cost of time-based investment can be tracked. Then the transition into the next stage of business development, namely of releasing the primary income producer into the consulting rooms, can take place more easily.

One way or another, unless you expect to invest something of yourself (time, money, commitment and emotion), you are not likely to succeed. It is helpful in this context to adjust your expectations by talking to other practitioners about their early experiences (most of us love talking about ourselves). Realistic expectations will lead you not to overestimate your potential income in terms of the number of counselling or training sessions you can undertake without suffering burnout. The more realistic you can be at this early stage of planning, the easier you will find it to survive after the glow and excitement of the honeymoon stage of business development have all but disappeared.

2.5 Your skills and interests

In addition to technical skills and professional competence in the relevant area of psychology, there are two other skill clusters that often determine whether a private practice will be successful. These are enterprise and business management. The enterprise aspect has to do with confident presentation of yourself and your business (selling yourself and loving it!), and the business management aspect includes strategy development, planning, administration, and financial management.

If these seem daunting and unfamiliar terms, there is no need to be alarmed as such skills can be acquired relatively easily as long as you are determined to acquire them. If you cannot locate such determination, it may be because your vocational interests simply do not lie in this area. This should not be a surprise: after all, you have chosen psychology as your profession.

Succeeding in private practice starts with a clear recognition of one's strengths and weaknesses, which in turn helps in the making of subsequent wise choices. Any lack of interest in business does not automatically disqualify you from running a private practice. You need to know your limits and compensate for them by seeking assistance of trusted professionals or choosing an alternative to a solo practice that demands the balancing act of three skill clusters (technical, human relations, and business). It may also be helpful to remember that the study of psychology involves all aspects of human behaviour, including running a professional business. Some of the cognitive skills that form a part of our repertoire for improving human performance can be very effectively applied to succeeding in private practice.

2.6 Adding options to solo practice

All too often, psychologists choose to start their practices on their own even though their mix of skills is incomplete. The result can be either an unexpected discovery of a hidden talent or, more likely, one of two often observed outcomes. The first is failure to sustain the practice in the long term. The second is an ongoing impoverished practice that, although financially unrewarding, is continued because of personal commitment or lack of other opportunities. At this early stage of considering entering private practice and conducting a personal skill audit, it is wise to consider alternatives to solo practice. Some such options are set out next.

2.6.1 Ask someone to join you

The most obvious alternative is to work with someone else who can complement your skills in the areas of marketing or business management. While this seems to be an easy option, the utmost care must be taken with the choice of a partner and with the drawing up of the necessary legal contract documentation. The concept of a legal partnership is addressed in more detail in the next chapter. It is useful to consider such an arrangement in its simplest form; that is, where everything is shared equally, including income, with the practitioners allocating time to the areas to which they are best suited.

Information about colleagues' interests and addresses is readily available in the British Psychological Society *Directory of Chartered Psychologists*. The Directory is a ready means of locating psychologists by both geographical area and speciality. It is envisaged that psychologists in private practice will have an entry in the Directory – a source that might be used by the public or by other professionals who might wish to locate someone of a particular speciality and geographical location. It contains more information about the practitioner than does the BPS's *Register of Chartered Psychologists*: apart from individual entries, there is an index to advertisers (individual entries), and a guide to speciality cross-tabulated by geographical location. However, the Register includes the names of all 8,600 or so Chartered Psychologists, including those who have chosen not to appear in the Directory. Its listing is by geographical location, but not by speciality. Both the Register and the Directory contain a copy of the BPS Code of Conduct.

Problems are bound to arise unless expectations of each other's roles and financial arrangements in the partnership are clearly articulated and formally agreed before starting. There can be no easier grounds for disagreement between partners than a perception that one party's financial reward is not commensurate with that party's effort. For example, most of the business might be generated by one partner, but both partners share the income equally; or one partner might have invested more time at the start of the practice because the other was still in full-time employment, and yet that extra effort is not reflected in the proportionate rewards. The effort that goes into marketing must also be adequately recognized and rewarded. This topic is further explored in the context of choosing a partnership as a business structure.

2.6.2 *Share the administrative load*

Another version of a joint practice – particularly useful when business management skills are scarce – is to enter an arrangement with another psychology practitioner whereby the administration is shared but the practices are separate. This model is akin to two medical practices where the reception area and all business systems are shared. The individual practitioners derive their separate incomes commensurate with the number of clients they see and the fees paid by those clients. The administration costs, which may include marketing of a practice, office-related costs, reception and support staff, etc., are shared, possibly equally, or in proportion to the business size of each practice, in relation to (for instance) the area occupied or the administrative effort utilized.

2.6.3 *Buy into an existing practice*

A more costly – but easier – option is to buy an existing psychology practice, or to buy a share in someone's established practice. In this way, all the administration systems would be expected to be in place and proven to be effective. To minimize the remaining risk inherent in such a decision, it is recommended to seek advice of a professionally qualified accountant with experience in auditing professional service businesses. This issue is tackled in more detail in Chapter 6, on selling your practice.

2.6.4 *Use other professionals' established systems*

Rather than buying into another psychologist's practice, a viable alternative may be to enter into some other kind of administration-sharing arrangement. This could be either renting a serviced office, or sharing with a professional whose business is other than psychology, in both of which cases there might already be the rooms and reception systems set up. This arrangement can take the form of a 'serviced office option' or an informal sub-leasing option. The practicalities of each of these options, such as expected costs, are covered elsewhere in this work.

The choice of a professional with whom administration could be shared would depend on your requirements for the client interface systems. Health professionals (chiropractors, medical specialists, physiotherapists, and general medical practitioners) would be most suitable for counselling or clinical psychology practices. Management consultants, business trainers, accountants or lawyers can also be potential administration-sharing partners, particularly for occupational psychologists.

One added advantage of such an arrangement is a potential for interdisciplinary client referrals and networking. Having other active and like-minded people around you where you work is a far better environment in which to succeed than sitting on your own in a home study.

There are other significant indirect benefits of sharing business administration with another professional, one of which is the presentation of a professional image to the clientele without prohibitive set-up costs. The feel of an established and successful practice should not be underestimated. It can be a very important factor in how positive you feel about the worth of your services, and that beneficial confidence may well flow into your marketing.

2.6.5 *Form a consortium*

Another variation on a partnership is a consortium of a number of psychologists, who pool their resources to set up their independent practices and collectively market them. Access to a larger pool of resources means that a marketing consultant can be hired, and (for example) 'glossy brochures' printed.

All the warnings about partnerships, which were sounded above, must be repeated for this option – this time using a loudspeaker! Given the nature of a consortium arrangement and an unpredictable workflow, some members may do very well while others may not have much work at all. The basis of income sharing must be meticulously addressed prior to starting such a venture, in order to avoid unnecessary pain and losses (in legal fees) after the initial glow and enthusiasm fade. It is strongly recommended that all arrangements involving partnerships, administration sharing, and consortia are constructed with the assistance of legal specialists.

2.7 Your attitude

From here on, this book will assume that you are ready to start a private psychology practice. So before plunging into a torrent of advice and practical hints, let us delve for a moment into your attitudes towards business, private practice, and earning income.

The authors offer no apology for their assumptions – which underpin this whole book – that a private practitioner is committed to quality of service. In this context, 'quality' means professionalism of the highest standard, a desire to continuously improve achieved standards, and unequivocal commitment to ethical behaviour. None of these commitments can be allowed to be subservient to the financial imperatives; that is, they cannot be traded for the desire to make more money. If this were to happen, the short-term gains would soon give way to long-term losses or underachievement.

The profession of psychology is young compared with, say, medicine and law, and public acceptance of a psychologist in private practice is even more recent. Therefore there is a collective responsibility on psychologists to ensure that the increasing credibility gained by, and trust placed in them is not undermined. Practices that do not measure up to the professional standards expected by our increasingly sophisticated society are to be avoided.

An important component of the attitude to quality and professionalism is the practitioner's belief in the intrinsic worth of the personal services being offered. If you are about to provide psychological 'products' to the marketplace, you must be assured that their quality is such that they are worth paying for.

It is said that the only difference between a business 'product' and a 'service' is that the former can be dropped on one's foot. It may therefore be more logical to refer to what psychologists do as 'service'. However, it might help to sharpen your thinking about your practice as a business to think of it in terms of providing tangible products. If we do not believe our product is worth buying or, worse, if the quality of the product is not up to scratch, we cannot seriously expect clients to purchase it, value it, recommend it, or help bring repeat business.

Another attitude that will become a determinant of your success is related to whether you think of your practice as a business, a lifestyle or a hobby. The ideal is a healthy balance of these concepts. It is vitally important that a practitioner has some insight into the fact that a business venture is being started. Such an attitude will direct your behaviour towards those areas that may not come intuitively to a psychologist, such as marketing plans, analysing balance sheets and cash flows. And yet there should also be an element to running the practice that brings enjoyment, just like a hobby.

2.8 Supervision

In its literal sense, supervision means overviewing or overseeing a person or operation. However, it has come to take on the meaning of being in charge, not always the most appropriate meaning for the practising professional. There are really two aspects to this issue: one is the internal and ongoing supervision of those working in the practice; the other is the periodic auditing of the practice by an outside expert. The first of these is carried out by the managing partner; the second is that of an outside expert performing an evaluation of the practice (see the subsections on 'Seeking professional advice' and 'The strategic audit' in Chapter 3).

Supervision of people in the practice depends on their role and status. The managing partner will be responsible for the supervision of non-professionals, whereas the supervision of peer colleagues is not of the same order. Where one might carefully supervise a recently-qualified professional employee, that role would not be appropriate for a partner or senior colleague. It is to this end that practice meetings are advised. The informal exchange of professional information, the discussion of cases, the development of a common philosophy, and the fostering of the collegial spirit are all beneficial – all this in addition to formal programs of external professional development (CPD – Continuing Professional Development).

The British Psychological Society has long required its members, including those in private practice, to have professional supervision in place. In the absence of such supervision, cases that come to the attention of the BPS's Investigatory Committee have attracted severely adverse attention. While there are no absolute rules about supervision, there are guiding principles. In addition to standard professional-practice guidelines, it is wise to consult experienced peer professionals from other practices (assuming that they are not adverse competitors).

Planning your practice

3.1 Choosing the market

'The market' is defined here as the group of people to whom you expect to sell your services. Your area of practice will be determined, in part, by your expertise, qualifications, experience and competence. If you have more than one speciality and find it difficult to decide which one to pursue in private practice, consider the profile, and therefore credibility, that you might enjoy in your potential marketplace. For example, you may be better known for your forensic work among solicitors, even though you are also competent at marriage counselling but have a much lower profile among a smaller clientele. It would be prudent to maximize the immediate potential income by concentrating first on the area in which the referrals are easiest to generate.

Whatever you do, the marketplace will tell you what it values. We have noted that practitioners think they excel in one speciality, but the referral pattern often shows that the marketplace values their skills in some other area. Your accounts will soon show you what the marketplace values. No matter what you think you are good at, the marketplace will send an unmistakable message. You may think that you are good at assessments, but the marketplace may tell you that you have a gift for phobia treatment, or personnel selection. In our experience, the marketplace tells you which of those things is financially rewarding.

In choosing your particular area of practice, you may also consider that the most profitable businesses seem to find their niche in the market and perfect those services to that niche rather than attempt to be 'everything to everyone'. Although it may contradict the conventional wisdom, there are plenty of stories about highly successful businesses that specialize in just one product. The downside of such a specialization could be the lack of professional development in other areas in which the practitioner also has an interest. The prospect of monotony has to be weighed against the need for speedy success.

In reality, psychologists tend to concentrate on more than one area to maintain their interest, motivation, and a reasonably broad referral base. Such a strategy also insures against the potential collapse of a one-income source. It should be noted, however, that claims of expertise in too many areas might be interpreted as expertise in none. The old joke that 'a client is anyone who is warm, vertical and has a chequebook' cannot be used as the basis of a successful enterprise.

The diversity of psychology as a profession is reflected in the many opportunities for private practitioners. By the time that psychologists are contemplating private practice, they will have no need of instruction about the various areas of psychology. Furthermore, the Divisions of the British Psychological Society are a guide to areas of speciality. The authors know of some successful practices that combine areas: organizational and educational, or forensic and clinical, for example.

3.2 Understanding your clients: market research

Market and social research organizations that are recognized for their research ability employ many psychologists. Those about to bet their future incomes on the success of their practices sometimes forget that they often possess the appropriate skills to research their markets before setting up. It is well known that if you want to succeed in anything in life, it helps if you plan it well; starting one's business is no different. After deciding on your area of practice, the next step must be to find out who your clients are, and what they need.

It pays to keep in mind at all times that the reason why your business exists is to service your clients. The concept of 'marketing' often gets bad publicity among the social-services professionals because of its confusion with selling. The perception is widespread that selling is somehow demeaning to a professional. Marketing is all about finding out what your clients need and planning ways to satisfy those needs.

While it is tempting to assume that you know what the market wants because of your knowledge of the industry or of the particular population on which you are focusing, it pays to check your assumptions. Conducting market research is a good way to do this, and it can be as simple or as expensive as you wish. (Be warned that the chances are that, even though you spend more on expert assistance in this area, it does not mean you get commensurate benefit.)

The following simple steps will make your market research as effective as you need it to be for the start of a small private practice. If you are planning a bigger venture, you may need to adjust this list or seek specialist market research advice. If you wish to reach other psychologists, the BPS pamphlet entitled *How to Reach Psychologists* is most useful. Consider the following:

- *Research existing data*. Locate as much currently available data about your clients and potential referrals as possible. This will include their views about psychologists, the types of problems experienced by your target population, how they tend to use such services, and other relevant issues. Useful sources of such data are the Office of National Statistics (website at <http://www.statistics.gov.uk.>), university libraries, local libraries, and colleagues from whom you can seek other potential sources of information.

- *Network with other practitioners*. An amazing amount of valuable knowledge can be amassed by asking other relevant practitioners about their experiences with clients and about their marketing initiatives. Most psychologists tend to freely share the information – as would most people when asked about their success. Make sure that you listen attentively and ask leading questions: 'How do you advertise?' 'How well do you find Yellow Pages works?' 'How do your clients find out about you?' Alternatively, if you come across a more talkative colleague, just ask a very open question such as: 'What has made your practice successful?' As a precondition, you must maximize the opportunities of meeting your counterparts, and so you should attend as many seminars, conferences, breakfasts, lunches, and professional development workshops as you can, specifically for the purpose of meeting other practitioners and particularly at the early stage of your career.

- *Ask your clients*. All too often, practitioners tend to forget that the best way of finding out about what the customers need is to ask them. A simple question at the beginning of the first session, such as 'Who suggested that you see me?', may be enough.

- *Use your own network of relevant friends or acquaintances*. For example, you may ask a general practitioner: `What would you find most useful from a psychologist?' or 'To what psychology services would you mostly refer your patients?' Human resource managers may be a useful source of information for the employee population: find out what they use psychologists for – selection assessments, psychological assessments, or employee counselling, for example. The next question you need to ask is: 'How can I make it easier for you to refer someone to me?'

- *Consider sample surveys of your target population* if your questions are still unanswered through informal means. Remember that the aim of market research is to define as precisely as possible the perceptions of the group of people with whom you would like to communicate about your practice. In the business of selling psychological products, there are usually two such groups: your direct clients, and the referrers of individual clients. Examples of two target groups are Human Resource/Personnel Managers (or line managers) actually benefiting from the service, and the executive decision-makers approving the expenditure. Since you would like to influence both groups via your brochures, phone calls, emails or letters, it is helpful to know as much as possible about both of them, especially in relation to their perceived needs for psychological intervention.

• *Conduct small trials for specific products*, as an alternative to formal market research surveys. If you would like to find out whether a particular product – for instance, a seminar or a group-therapy session – is acceptable to the market, it may be more cost-effective to advertise it and test the response rather than ask questions about it in a survey. The advantage of this approach is that if your intuition is right, you will have an immediate number of clients who sign up as a measure of its success. As a consequence, your 'market research' (advertising) costs will have been recovered, and possibly some profit made. The obvious disadvantage is that you need to rely on your guesses as to what is an acceptable product. You must also be aware of the risk of failing to attract a reasonable number of responses, in which case you may have to face the unpleasant consequences of cancelling the event and returning cheques to potential clients.

The fundamental principle of conducting your market research is to find out what your clients need and how best to package the product so that they will wish to purchase it. You need to know precisely how clients can be assisted in seeking your service or making referrals to you. Everything else that follows in the development of private practice will depend on this information, from writing marketing brochures through to preparing reports. The use of market research extends beyond increasing client referrals. It can also help choose the right position and area of operation for the practice. For a tabular approach see Appendix A.

3.3 Choosing the location

The geographical location of your practice will probably be dependent on the area of speciality catered for by your practice, the type of clientele you have, the image you desire to portray, and affordability. The results of your market research should have provided you with valuable information on where your clients are most likely to be located. This will include whether being close to public transport links is important, and how many other psychologists already operate in your geographical proximity.

The conventional wisdom about not setting up businesses too close to competitors does not always apply to psychological practices. There are some notable examples in the metropolitan cities where a number of psychological practices co-exist very successfully in close proximity. This is also observed in other service professions, e.g., law and finance.

Whatever your choice, you must consider your clients' perception of your practice location, particularly if you expect them or their referrers to visit your premises. The choice of various venues, with a discussion on their advantages and disadvantages to consider, is presented in more detail elsewhere in this work.

3.4 Choosing the business structure

3.4.1 Considering your needs

The choice of a business structure from which your practice will operate depends in the main on your personal financial situation, your taxation position, and your preferences. The chosen business or legal structure will be the entity through which your business trades with the external world, namely your clients and your suppliers. You will also need to comply with various government regulations, corresponding to the structure you have chosen.

There are three general types of structures from which you will have to choose to run your practice:

- unincorporated structures such as sole trader or partnership;
- an incorporated company;
- a trading trust.

Although it is vital to consult a professional business adviser or an accountant before making a final decision, it pays to be prepared. One form that this preparation might take is that of reading this present handbook carefully and making your own list of questions. Accounting language can be rather specialized, and with the added complexity of the taxation system the choices and implications may seem daunting.

Apart from the brief discussion that follows, there are small-business publications and information centres that may provide valuable resources at this early stage of business planning. A list of useful addresses is given in Appendix B. Further, as mentioned earlier, the major banks offer business starter kits that are very good indeed. Among other things they contain useful summaries of what an entrepreneur should incorporate into a business plan. Clearly, banks have in mind the acquisition of new customers, and that is a worthy motive so long as they provide a good professional service to those customers.

The choice of a legal structure you will make at this stage is likely to have significant implications for your practice in the future. The form may not be easily changed because of capital gains implications, so choose carefully. For example, if you were to decide that your trading trust or partnership should become a limited liability company, you might face expenses and taxes because the new company will immediately be of value even though no cash has been generated. This value is derived from the company being an entity that now exists ready for trading, with inbuilt goodwill and the labour and expense that have gone into its construction.

Some of the questions you may consider in making your choices are related to your long-term vision for the practice and your personal circumstances. For example:

- Are you planning to operate on your own or do you hope to expand by asking other practitioners to join you?
- What is your realistic income target, and can you generate it on your own?
- Do you hope to expand by employing other psychologists and/or support staff?
- If your practice generates a substantial profit, who would you like to benefit from your proportion of it – you, your family, and/or charitable organizations?
- Would you like to provide incentives to others, such as your staff, by profit sharing?
- Would you like to invite others to purchase part of the business by injecting capital into it?

Depending on your answer to these and similar questions, one structure may have obvious advantages. In general, if you plan to work on your own, sole trading may suffice; if you hope to employ others, a company may be more appropriate; if profit sharing among the family or staff is a high consideration on your list, a trading trust may be a better option. In relation to this last option, the flexibility can be attractive to distribute profit in a discretionary way among either family members or non-profit organizations. On a cautionary note, however, this use of trusts is very complex and so professional advice is essential.

3.4.2 Sole trading

The simplest and most immediate way of operating a business is as a sole trader, using your own name or initials. If you use your own name, check that there is no requirement to register it as a business.

In this scenario, you must keep good records for tax purposes. Failure to deal appropriately with Inland Revenue can be costly in terms of money, time, and reputation – all this of course apart from the impropriety of not conforming to received standards. On the positive side, the Inland Revenue can be very helpful to those trying to operate to high standards. Its staff provide, amongst other things, regular workshops run by Business Support Teams, and they give advice on an individual basis. They also are bound by what they call 'Customer Service Standards', in which they set out their criteria of prompt, efficient, and courteous service. The Inland Revenue's targets are outlined in measurable terms (e.g., calculating tax correctly every time, telephone calls answered within 30 seconds, speed of responding by post, etc.).

Changing from being an employee to a sole trader involves clarifying the position with both the Department of Social Security (DSS) and the Inland Revenue. As there are tax advantages in being a sole trader as distinct from an employee, those bodies may scrutinize the arrangement to ensure that the 'sole trader' appellation is not just an employee in disguise. There are four tests that determine status: they are known as the 'mutual obligations' test, the 'control' test, the 'integration' test, and the 'economic reality' test. Discuss these criteria with your expert adviser.

3.4.3 Trading under a business name

A more popular and just as inexpensive way of commencing a UK business is to register a business name with Companies House in Cardiff. This action allows you to nominate any name – which may include your name or initials – as long as it has not been already registered by someone else and it is not subject to other restrictions imposed by law. The essence here is that a company name should not be such as to be 'passed off' as being that of another trading entity. Further, among the legal restrictions are those that prevent a business name being tasteless and trivializing, that implies a connection with the government or a local authority, or that uses the word 'Royal'; there are terms that are restricted for some other reasons as well. Three examples of inappropriate titles are: 'Condomaniacs, The Sex Therapists'; 'Guaranteed Results Consulting' [professional work is on a fee-for-service basis – not on outcome]; and 'British Royal Psychology Practice'.

The process of registering a business name is quite simple and not time consuming. Visiting the appropriate government authority with a list of preferred business names usually accomplishes it. Business-registration application forms are available, and it is possible to search the Internet for names already registered. This self-search will save time, ensuring that the name has not already been registered. The fee for registering a business name is considerably less than that for registering a limited liability company, but the costs of registering a limited liability company are lower if one does it oneself. A half-way stage is to buy a company set up with the express purpose of being sold to potential users. Such companies have never traded, and so have no debts or liabilities. As they are kept in store ('on the shelf') waiting for a purchaser, they are called 'shelf companies'.

When you have completed the formalities, an official registration certificate will be sent to you and there are requirements to display this certificate in a prominent place at the business location.

Operating under a registered business name requires only those annual returns normally prepared for taxation return purposes. The obvious advantage of sole trading or business name registration is the low cost of set-up and ongoing maintenance of such a structure. Any losses may be offset against other income, and PAYE (pay-as-you-earn) tax does not have to be paid if the proprietors draw cash from the business, although tax on drawings from the business (which count as personal income) must be paid in twice-yearly instalments.

It is relatively easy to transfer the business constituted under a business name to another legal structure at a later stage, although there may be capital gains tax implications. You will be charged capital gains tax if you make a profit of over £7,100 when disposing of a capital asset (as at March 2000, and after allowing for inflation).

The main disadvantage of sole trading under your own or business name is that it is difficult to maintain the business in the event of retirement, disablement or death of the main owner of the business. The owner is also personally responsible for all the business liabilities (debt, contracts, leases, etc.). It needs also to be noted, however, that personal responsibility applies to a large extent in all structures. The thrust of company legislation aims increasingly at the accountability of the directors of companies and the trustees of trusts. Thus, while your personal responsibility for business liabilities needs to be taken into account when choosing a business structure, it cannot be the overriding factor. You must make yourself fully aware of the extent of your responsibilities, especially when you enter into leasing or other borrowing arrangements that include your personal guarantees.

3.4.4 Partnership

A partnership exists where two or more people are in business together and share the profits (and losses). Where there is no formal agreement, the situation comes under the Partnership Act 1890. A partnership as a business structure is very similar to a sole trader status in terms of its legal requirements. Apart from the requirements to register the business name, and timely notification to the Inland Revenue, there are no other expenses and formalities associated with this structure. The liability of the partners is not limited, as it is in a limited liability company.

The critical aspect of operating under partnership is the choice of a partner and the formal agreement. It is highly recommended that a specific agreement be drawn up, using professional assistance from a solicitor, to be sure that all eventualities and issues have been clearly documented and agreed. In the absence of such an agreement, the rules of the partnership will be subject to the law operating at the time. While there are many examples of successful relationships between partners based on mutual trust and cooperation, it is wise not to assume that such a relationship will continue.

There are many parallels between a business partnership and marriage. In both cases, the choice of a partner starts the relationship (often on the basis of other than rational arguments), which needs careful development, nurturing, negotiation and compromises if it is to survive. A business partnership is similarly tested most severely in both financial extremes – lean and rich times. When the going gets tough, there is pressure to perform better and to generate more income. During this phase, particularly in the early stages of partnership, there is sufficient enthusiasm to insulate the relationship from friction.

There are parallels here with franchise operations. This initial stage has been creatively described by Nathan (1993) as 'the glee stage', where you are both excited about the new venture and full of hope for the future. When there are plentiful profits and the time comes to distribute them, the little-researched human characteristic colloquially referred to as greed tends to interfere with the previously existing harmony in the relationship. The partnership is then likely to enter 'the me stage' (Nathan, 1993), where you may start to think: 'I could probably be just as successful without you'. It is easy to imagine, for example, a scenario where one partner's efforts (for instance, a seminar or a specific marketing campaign) generated a substantial profit that was not commensurate with the personal efforts of all partners. This situation must be foreseen, and clear procedures and expectations should be documented. In fact, the details of all rules governing the behaviour of partners must be precisely articulated, so as to avoid pain and disappointment not to mention legal costs or broken relationships.

Not surprisingly, consistent ethical behaviour by all parties is the most significant determining factor in a successful partnership. If you are seriously considering a partnership structure as the basis for your business, it is worthwhile to emulate other successful models of such practices, both in psychology and in other professions (such as law or medicine). Take time to find out how others have solved their difficulties and developed their agreements.

It is important to remember that the partners as joint business owners are personally responsible for all the liabilities of the business. This is particularly important to consider when taking out a loan on a 'joint and several' basis, in which case if one partner fails to meet the required repayments, creditors are likely to seek the funds from other partners. Another disadvantage of a partnership structure is its lack of flexibility in transferring ownership to others.

A partnership agreement will need to include:

- the names of the partners and the trading name;
- what the business does and what its scope is;
- the business address;
- capital contributions and entitlements;
- the time to be devoted to the business;
- the arrangements for sharing profit and loss;
- arrangements for cash withdrawals;
- banking arrangements;
- personal accounts and how they are to be kept and monitored;
- the allocation of duties;
- the allocation of decision making;
- the duration of the partnership agreement;
- conditions that will apply if the partnership is dissolved;
- conditions of sale of the partnership or sale of part of the partnership;
- admission arrangements for new members to the partnership;
- the retirement or death of a partner;
- expulsion or compulsory retirement;
- any restrictions on partners;
- various insurances both corporate and personal.

Although there are substantial benefits to partnerships, there are also grave dangers. The formality of a partnership is not always in accord with its social dynamics. It is worth emphasizing that a partnership agreement should be understood as an arrangement between consenting parties who do not necessarily trust each other. There are two real-life illustrative stories here.

One concerns a psychologist and an economist/accountant who teamed up together to provide a service to business. They knew and trusted each other, and worked in a complementary fashion. The economist/accountant ran the business side of things and did consultation accounts; the psychologist also did consultation accounts and devoted the remainder of his time to developing intellectual property for their partnership. This burgeoning consulting business became profitable in its own right. Additionally, the intellectual property (the tracking of marketing strategies) was franchised in several countries. The partners then profitably sold the consulting company and retained ownership of the intellectual property – and its income. From beginning to selling took just over 10 years. Both partners are now developing their interests in new directions and find life fulfilling. It is pleasing to record that they remain firm friends.

The second story concerns two psychologists who formed a practice partnership. They had full and frank discussions of how it would operate, set out the principles in plain prose, had the bank account in joint signatures, took legal advice, etc. That partnership foundered on the personalities of the partners. The formalities were agreed but the 'who did most and how profitable was it, who gives the administrative directions' etc. became sticking points. Although the partners agreed on the principles of the practice, their life views were grossly disparate. Eventually one partner sold his share to the other and left the practice entirely – the poorer for it and sadly experienced.

Of all of the cases known to the authors of this book, the ones that work best are those in which trust and liking have been developed prior to forming a partnership. In these cases, the partnership is an extension of an already felicitous relationship. Above all else, the twin qualities of trust and generosity of spirit are paramount in a partnership. As such, the authors suggest the greatest caution before forming or joining a partnership.

3.4.5 A limited liability company

A limited liability company is a legal entity or structure. It can make contracts, own property, sue or be sued, and even continue to exist where there has been a change of ownership. The documents that govern the functioning of a company are called its Memorandum and Articles of Association. The officers of the company must meet the Companies Acts of 1985 and 1989. There must be a director and a company secretary (who may also be a director but cannot be a sole director). There is limitation of liability, but some dealings with small companies may involve the director(s) giving personal guarantees.

There are two ways of obtaining a company: forming a new company or purchasing one 'off the shelf'. Shelf companies are already registered, ready with all appropriate documents of constitution, and are available from agents, accountants or solicitors. The original registered name is then changed to a suitable name chosen by the purchaser of the shelf company before being registered with Companies House in Cardiff, which issues an appropriate certificate. An accountant or commercial solicitor can advise and guide you through the necessary steps in either process. You can obtain direct services from a solicitor or agents listed in *Yellow Pages* under 'Company Registration Agents'. Shelf companies should be obtainable for under £150 (in early 2000). That is rather more expensive than the option of doing it yourself (costing about £20). If there is more than one owner, the Memorandum and Articles of Association needed before the company trades will probably raise the costs.

As any director of a company will probably be a shareholder, a director can also act as company secretary. It is assumed here that the company is private and not public. (Public Limited Companies – PLCs – are listed on a stock exchange, which usually takes place when finance is raised from the public issue of shares. Such a step is significantly more involved and requires professional assistance.) When a private company issues shares, these are allotted by its directors, who also approve transfers of subscribers' shares, according to their minuted decisions in board meetings. Directors of companies are liable for what the company does. As such they bear a burden of responsibility which they might wish to protect by the purchase of directors' professional indemnity insurance.

Further shares can be issued at a determined value to another person when an injection of finance is required. When someone invests in a company, there is usually an expectation of a return on their investment. Each year, a company's profit is assessed for the availability of funds to be distributed as a dividend to shareholders. It is important to note that dividends are paid out of profit or accumulated profit, and not out of capital. Thus a company that is not profitable is of little value to its shareholders unless they can count on its capital value improving when they are ready to sell their shares.

A company cannot trade until a certificate of incorporation has been issued. As soon as the (new) owner receives all the documentation, that owner will have to hold the first meeting of directors, as required by the Articles of Association. In fact, there are requirements for holding *regular* meetings of directors, for which official minutes must be kept. This, and many other requirements, do not have to be daunting if your accountant continues to provide you with ongoing professional services to ensure that you comply with all the company regulations.

There are costs associated with compliance with the requirements of Companies House, which have to be taken into account in addition to the initial set-up costs. These include both direct government charges for annual company returns, and indirect costs associated with accounting services. The former costs are fixed, but professional fees are negotiated with your accountant and these will depend upon the amount of work involved.

There are some further disadvantages of company structures, other than high initial costs. Company losses cannot be distributed to the shareholders to be offset against their other income. There is also the often forgotten problem with companies limited by shares, where a number of psychologist–shareholders commence practising together with little initial capital outlay. If their venture becomes profitable, the company share price will have increased dramatically even though no actual money was paid. If one shareholder would like to sell shares, the purchase of one's own business is likely to cost a substantial sum of money that may not actually be available from the business. In such a case, another person may need to be found to purchase those shares.

While it is easy to focus on the disadvantages of operating a practice under a company structure, there are also significant advantages. First, taxation on company profits is at significantly lower rates compared with the maximum personal marginal rate. After-tax profits can be retained in business for further expansion. And the liabilities of a company are limited to that company. This last advantage needs to be qualified since the directors may also be personally responsible for debt, which the company cannot repay, especially if the directors have given personal guarantees for business loans or overdrafts. Two further advantages are that it is relatively easy to increase ownership in a company, and to continue trading when the founders can no longer work.

All such possibilities need to be explored with your accountant. Do not be satisfied with simple and immediate advice on what legal structure your practice requires. This needs to be considered in the light of your future personal, professional and financial goals, for which the business structure should become a vehicle not a prison.

3.4.6 Cooperatives

This form of commercial operation may take a variety of forms and requires expert advice. While there are several distinct advantages in cooperatives, the complexities sound a warning note to those contemplating this form of business structure.

3.4.7 Trusts

It seems that the least understood (at least, by psychologists) business structures are trusts, which may take a variety of forms. In essence, the most common use of a trust is as a financial vehicle for a family. In some forms of trust there might be elements of discretion as to how the income is distributed, and it might involve benefits to members of the trust who are minors or non-working spouses. Some trusts might trade, while others may not do so. There are clear implications here for the balancing of costs, distribution of income, spreading of losses, and the general aim of being in practice. Before talking to your financial adviser you will need to be clear about your aims. As with company structures, trusts may have profit shares or units, voting shares or units, and capital shares or units. This flexibility may be advantageous in some circumstances – for instance, adding and deleting trust members as circumstances change, bearing in mind the commercial advantages as well as the family advantages. Added to this there is the potential advantage of using this distinction for valuable employees or subcontractors.

Among the disadvantages of trust structures is the inability to distribute losses that can be offset against the beneficiaries' other income, and the costs associated with ongoing administration and compliance with government regulations. Both of these disadvantages are common to limited companies as well. In addition, banks or other creditors usually demand evidence from solicitors that trusts have been properly constituted and that no changes to their Articles of Association have occurred, which at worst causes minor inconvenience and delays the proceedings.

3.4.8 Seeking professional advice

When selecting a business structure from those outlined above, or any other alternative, it is strongly recommended that you seek your accountant's advice. There is also much government-sponsored free (or quite cheap) advice and published material from business support centres and government publishing bookshops (see Appendix B for further resources).

An appointment with an accountant should come first, but there is no reason to accept the accountant's initial suggestion, especially if all the implications and terminology are not clear. Ask lots of questions and seek other opinions as part of your initial research. Different business structures suit different people, and there are many different psychologists. You need to evaluate all the costs, taxation implications and alternatives, to be able to make an informed decision that will suit your needs. When you are evaluating the pros and cons of the options, make sure that you consider your long-term plans, not just the immediate set-up costs.

There are many accountants who specialize in helping business enterprises start and grow, and so it makes sense to choose a professional accountant who has a proven track record with this type of business, rather than someone who has the lowest charge rates or who is a family friend. Among the considerations in choosing an accountant will be a personal recommendation from someone whose judgement you trust. Their qualifications (and membership of an appropriate professional body), the price of their services, their location, what specialities they offer, their general reputation, whether your personal styles are compatible and, possibly, whether they operate in a 'one-stop shop' with professionals from complementary professions (e.g., lawyers, financial advisers) are each important considerations.

Your accountant will probably refer you to a solicitor, and possibly a financial planner, for further specialist advice, according to your changing requirements. It should be remembered, nevertheless, that nobody will actually know your business as well as you do. No accountant can be expected to cast visions for your business. Only you can do that, and it is quite likely that if you are high on enterprise skills you already have future visions for your practice.

The Law Society has produced a pamphlet (1999) entitled *Lawyers for your Business: Succeed in Business, the Legal Angle*. That pamphlet lists the kinds of issues and problems that solicitors help to solve. The Law Society is contactable via its website (see Appendix B).

During meetings with professionals, it is helpful to be aware of the advantages and drawbacks of each method of trading. Being a sole trader is easy, flexible, and can employ family members – but if it fails then personal possessions are at risk, it ceases on the death of the owner, and it is sometimes considered to be of lower prestige. Partnership has the advantages of collecting people of complementary skills, of minimum legal procedures, of continuity if a partner is absent or ill, and being a forum for the discussion of common professional interests; the drawbacks are that if the business fails, each partner is liable for all of the business debts, the actions of one partner bind all of the others, and intractable disagreements may occur – leading to ill will (and possible failure of the partnership). Limited companies do just that: they limit financial liability. They have a separate and continuing existence independent of the individual members, shares are easily transferable, rewards in salary and shares can be arranged, they are likely to have greater prestige, and there are some tax advantages. Against this is the fact that they are more expensive to set up and to run, the rules to be followed under the Companies Acts must be followed strictly, and losses in early years cannot be offset against other income. There is no way of determining which is the best structure in any particular case, but what has been set out in this part of the handbook might help focus discussion with your advising professionals.

3.5 Developing a business plan

There are many useful skills and aspects of knowledge that psychologists bring to business management from their standard academic training, although many are not aware of them because their application is in a different context. Counselling psychologists have technical skills in helping their clients formulate their personal development action plans; vocational psychologists advise on career plans; organizational psychologists help with change-management strategies. All psychologists are aware of the cognitive processes, the power of language and visualization, which together determine a person's effectiveness. Preparing a business plan utilizes all of those skills and concepts.

Effective business plans have just as much to do with these psychological concepts as do financial and management skills. Successful business people have learned the power of planning, envisioning the future, and of evaluating strengths and weaknesses. They also undertake business planning on a regular basis, usually once a year. As mentioned previously, readers may find valuable programmes available from the major banks; ask for a business starter kit. Those viewed by the authors are deemed very good indeed. In the packages are leaflet explanations, information pamphlets, and (generally) a diskette or CD-ROM (see section 4.11.2 below) with a business plan, posing pertinent questions and formalizing answers. If your attitude is such that you would rather not become involved in such 'mundane' activity, a more realistic option for you may be to remain in employment or at least join with others – do not start your business alone.

3.5.1 Why a business plan?

Businesses that begin with a written and realistic plan are less likely to fail within the first years of operation. This should be the first step in the commencement of a professional psychology practice and then at least an annual event. If you fail to plan, you probably plan to fail. You might have said that yourself in a different context, but it is just as applicable to running a practice. While it is easier to begin 'doing' things rather than planning them, the danger of underplanning is that you spend your time ineffectively – when things get busier you will be involved in so many urgent things that you will not have time to spend on the important ones.

Formulating a business plan is one of those activities of the 'Non-Urgent but Important' quadrant (Covey, 1993), as presented in Figure 3.1 below. Its value is often appreciated much later when you evaluate how you spend your time. An immediate and tangible reason why you will find a business plan useful is that bank managers and accoun-

Figure 3.1: Time management matrix

	Urgent	**Not urgent**
Important	Quadrant 1 Crises Deadlines Pressing problems	Quadrant 2 Planning Relationship building Recreation
Not important	Quadrant 3 Phone interruptions Some mail Some meetings/reports	Quadrant 4 Trivia Time wasters Some phone calls

Source: Adapted from Covey (1993)

tants will find it much easier to understand your practice and to evaluate your needs when you present them with a plan that speaks their language.

There are also some less tangible effects that a business plan will have on your practice, even though you never show it to anyone, and even if you yourself do not read it every day. Writing down your cognitive constructs, articulating your vision, and planning your goals is a powerful way of focusing and directing your behaviour towards your identified goals.

To summarize, here are some benefits of formulating a business plan:

- it focuses your vision for the practice;
- it forces you to clearly identify your products;
- it serves to evaluate your thoughts and ideas;
- it helps shape your practice's long-term future;
- it helps in your communication with financial advisers;
- it ensures your resources are spent efficiently;
- it instils confidence in your practice – for both those outside and those inside the practice;
- it minimizes costly mistakes;
- it provides a basis for measuring your performance.

3.5.2 What is a business plan?

A business plan is a document that provides a description of your practice, and concludes with very specific strategies and action points, including financial details. The five simple questions (Samson, 1988) that a business plan purports to answer are:

1. Where are we now?
2. What business are we in?
3. Where do we want to be in the future?
4. What changes are necessary to close the gap between the now and the future?
5. How do we make it happen?

Its contents, described in more detail in the following sections, generally comprise:

- an executive summary;
- a situational analysis;
- a strategic audit;
- some short-term and long-term objectives;
- business strategies (covering marketing, professional services, and financial control);
- an implementation plan;
- performance evaluation.

Although it is recommended that you involve someone else to provide a helpful and evaluative sounding board, you cannot expect that other person to formulate your business plan for you. You are the only one who knows the answers to the questions that the plan forces you to answer. You might employ specialist business advisers to write the document, but do not be surprised when, at the end of the exercise, you wonder why you paid so much money for someone to write down what you yourself said.

A cost-efficient approach to writing a business plan is to write its first draft by yourself and then present it to someone with business and financial skills (for instance, your accountant). Be prepared to answer all the challenges and questions put to you. Presentation of your plan, your thoughts and strategies is greatly enhanced when someone skilled in business planning assesses it with some independence and objectivity. The notes below provide a general guide. Detailed business plans, as has been mentioned, are available in the starter kits obtainable from major banks.

3.5.3 Business plan contents

Set out next is further guidance on the elements of a typical business plan.

Executive summary
Most bank managers or other creditors are not likely to read the entire document, and so it is good business practice to produce a summary

of key statements and indicators in a one-page executive summary. This summary may include sections such as:

- historical background;
- vision and mission statements;
- target market and product/service description;
- key objectives and strategies;
- key financial indicators and future estimates.

Situational analysis
This section is most relevant to businesses already in practice and may include the following:

- **Historical background.** This includes the details surrounding the commencement of the practice, such as who founded it and when.

- **Products/services.** Probably the most fundamental aspect of any business and often rather difficult for psychologists whose services are not tangible, it defines, usually through a 'mission statement', the types of services that your practice intends to provide.

- **The target market.** Covers defining your clients and describing them in more detail so as to specify what their needs are and to what extent your products will meet their needs.

- **The total market.** This is an assessment consisting of some guesses but also possibly based on available population and market research statistics. This section provides information on the entire market available to the practice. For a look at unofficial statistical sources, Mort (1990) is a good starting point.

    If, for instance, it is a counselling/clinical practice, how many people per year do you expect will need your types of services in your defined geographical area? If it is an organizational practice, how many organizations are likely to require your type of services? Consider how much each client is likely to pay for such a service; this will provide you with the total value of the market in which you are about to operate. You should perform this calculation for each of the types of products/services you plan to provide.

    The information gleaned from this exercise will provide you with an objective estimate of the total potential amount available in your market. Considering that other practitioners will already operate in your area of practice and geographical proximity, the next question is how your services and market (your clientele) relate to those of the other providers (your competitors).

- *Other providers*. While it is counterintuitive for psychologists to think of their professional colleagues as 'competitors', it is worthwhile to consider them as such for the purposes of planning your services. Consider whether your services are similar to or different from theirs. Are your potential clients (your target market) overlapping theirs, or is the market distinctly different? If you are planning to provide existing services to the same market, you will be essentially aiming at cutting into their share of the available market.

  Fortunately, in the current climate of the need for psychology services, there are constantly expanding markets and there is potential to provide services that at this stage are not available, and so the issue of competition is not a seriously limiting factor for psychology practices. It is probable that in the foreseeable future the number of services will expand to the point where the practitioners will seriously have to consider the market share they are planning to absorb.

- *Market research*. It is nevertheless a worthwhile exercise to think of business planning, and about others providing a similar service to yourself. A simple search for various advertisers in the newspapers and *Yellow Pages*, informal networking, and formal market research will all serve to uncover the colleagues against whom you will be potentially competing for business. This analysis is significant for at least two reasons: geographical location and quality comparison. First, it is useful to be aware of other psychologists operating in geographical proximity, so that when potential clients (or referrers of clients) mention another psychologist's name you will not appear surprised. Second, it will help you understand how another practitioner operates. This will provide a useful benchmark against which you can measure the quality of your services. This may also lead you to develop a product that clearly distinguishes you from others.

- *Structure*. Describes how your business is organized. Initially this may be a simple statement or a one-line description of all the functions you will be performing. As your business grows, this will probably become more complex. It is worthwhile to identify at least the different functions that your private practice has to perform to operate as a business. These include:
  - professional services;
  - finance;
  - administration;
  - personnel; and
  - marketing. .

Each of these functions has to be managed so that your practice can run efficiently. In a small practice, it is common for some of these functions to be performed by the same person, by external service providers such as a typist/computer operator, or by part-time and casual staff who provide assistance as needed and charge at an hourly rate.

The structure also has to do with the management of each function, rather than its operation, and so the questions you need to answer are: who is operating, and who is responsible for these functions?

- **Resources**. Describes the sources of all the business needs. The primary resource in a psychology-based business is the professional human resource. You will begin to think here about the people who need to provide the services that are the fundamental product(s) that your business sells. While in most practices this will be provided by yourself, also consider staff, subcontractors, or locums. Collaboration with another practice group can be helpful, when the workload exceeds your capacity to perform the services or when you are unavailable – for example, when you are on holiday or attending a conference.

  Human resources must also be considered for all the other functions described in the structure above. Who will, for example, assist in appointments, respond to calls, perform administration and financial management when you are not available?

  Other resources include premises from which the practice operates and suppliers providing you with the essentials for operating your business.

- **Technology**. Comprises machinery, computers, telephones, communication equipment, computer software, and psychological test materials. At this point you will identify the current technology that your practice utilizes in its operation.

Strategic audit

This section of the business plan is essentially a critical analysis of how your practice is currently performing. Business management experts have borrowed the concept of a SWOT (Strengths, Weaknesses, Opportunities and Threats) analysis from group facilitators – most likely psychologists! Value may be achieved by standing back, by using someone else to talk things through, and by writing down your thoughts and conclusions. This calls for some insight into your personal qualities as well, given that psychology-practice products are usually so intricately linked to the person delivering them.

A SWOT analysis provides the following:

- *Strengths* – identifying the services at which your practice excels. You will ask yourself here what you do in your practice that is better than, or different from, anyone else.

- *Weaknesses* – listing the aspects of your practice that others do better. You need to honestly assess the areas that you feel need improving.

- *Opportunities* – presenting the untapped potential that your practice has not explored. You will become aware of the areas of service that are not provided by anyone within your market, or new markets for your existing services.

- *Threats* – including all the factors that work against the viability of your practice. These may consist of internal limitations or external pressures, local issues or global government actions. It is far better to consider the threats and face them, so that you can consciously turn them into opportunities.

You can complete the SWOT analysis for the overall practice or separately under various areas of your practice performance, such as the service, marketing, resources or finances. You will need to be aware of the actual performance in each of these areas before being able to proceed to formulate strategies for improvement and growth.

Vision and mission statements
In formulating a 'vision statement', you will find it helpful to imagine where you would like to see your practice at the end of a reasonably long period of time – say five or 10 years. The vision statement should succinctly articulate your practice's philosophy and purpose. One way to begin thinking about such a statement is to try to find an answer to: 'My practice exists to …'. The simpler and more precise a statement, the more beneficial.

The practice's 'mission statement' must also be clearly spelt out in the business plan. This can be either at its beginning or here in the strategic audit section. Mission statements have been abused by many in the business world and some have written them simply because everyone else seems to have done so. Those who put substantial effort into formulating such statements have demonstrated their power. It should be a simple and individual statement, which motivates and focuses you and those working with you on the activities that really matter in your practice. Do not be afraid to alter and edit the mission statement in the next business-planning cycle. Some examples are as follows:

- 'Our aim is assisting individuals in resolving personal problems in the workplace in small to medium-sized manufacturing organizations.'
- 'This practice provides forensic assessments for a group of clinical psychologists.'
- 'We give psychological advice to personnel selection agencies.'
- 'We are in the business of improving individual performance of athletes competing in [named sport].'

Strategies

It will be seen that the vision statement is an expression of high-level aspiration: the mission statement is a more practical statement which spells out how that vision is to be achieved.

Each business has its unique factor that enables it to exist in a sustained way. This special capacity for ongoing business viability of a practice probably has a lot to do with the psychologist's competence. The business success goes beyond the individual's capability – it also has to do with the way the practice is marketed and the way in which service is delivered. This section articulates the strategies which will ensure the ongoing viability of the business.

It is important to decide what type of private practice you would like to operate: a single provider relying for all income on the exertion of one person; a two-person, three-person practice; or a consulting group. In general, there are four options for business growth:

- provision of more existing services into the existing markets;
- development of new services for the existing markets;
- location of new markets for the existing services;
- development of new services for new markets.

The 'markets' here mean client groups and/or referrers of such clients, or projects for psychology practices. Your statement of the basis for growth (or sustainability) will therefore articulate your general objective as to how you plan to continue to run a viable practice. This may, for example, entail developing new products (seminars, specialist counselling or consulting services) for a new group of clients (defined by their location, a demographic characteristic, or belonging to a type of organization).

The strategies presented below specifically address how you should plan to achieve something like the above general objective. They comprise:

- marketing strategy;
- service strategy;
- resource strategy;
- financial strategy.

Marketing strategy

A marketing strategy is one of the most powerful elements of the business plan and will be addressed again in more detail in Chapter 4. If you have identified in your growth objective that you will develop a new psychology product or target a new group of clients, this is the place where you will write down how you plan to ensure that these clients use your services. Some of the aspects you may like to cover in this strategy are:

- position in the market (describing your practice image, tone and 'feel', and how you plan to achieve it – how you would like others to think of your practice);
- target market for each service (describing each group as precisely as you can, drawing upon knowledge gained from market research);
- range of products/services you plan to provide (presenting an analysis of the profit margin that each product is expected to contribute out of total sales, or, if it is a clearly identifiable product such as a training seminar, a break-even analysis);
- fee-setting approach (describing how you plan to arrive at the fees you will charge for each product);
- marketing activities (detailing how you will communicate about your products to existing or new client groups – by direct mail, advertising, promotion, free seminars, etc.).

In your planning of marketing strategies you may come across the concept of 'elasticity of demand', which derives from economics and refers to a variability of purchasing when the goods or services vary in price. Some caution is needed here because, in professional work, fee lowering may produce an unintended effect. Some people believe that the more they pay (within reason) the better the product, and so the value you put on your services may, in part, determine public perceptions of what you offer. What you can do is provide something extra – such as a novel service, a conventional service in an underserviced location, flexibility of consulting times, or an array of services acting in concert.

One successful marketing strategy is to find a niche market. An unfulfilled need at the intersection of two areas or issues can become a thriving business. Examples are: the clinical treatment of the fear of flying for people travelling on business; the software servicing of research computers; behavioural-management strategies for the families of autistic children; and negotiation skills, property settlements, and life plans for divorcing couples. There may be a niche market appropriate for your situation, but consider whether there is a *sufficient* market in the identified niche (how many clients, and how much continuing business?) to make entry financially justifiable. It is worth emphasizing that a good reputation in such approaches takes a while to establish.

Service strategy

In relation to service strategy, although it is expected that professionals in private practice are skilled and competent to provide their services, you will need to convince others (bank managers, for example) that you have that capacity and that you have planned contingencies if you are unable to provide those services yourself. It is useful to consider in this respect the following: the skills of those who will provide the services; the location from which the services will be provided; the frequency and scheduling of the services; the quality assurance of the services; and the safety of clients.

Resource strategy

The resource strategy will address human resources required for the practice, but in areas other than direct service provision. It will decide who will perform the functions of administration, office/clinic management, reception, accounting, cleaning, and such like. Other resources, including the rooms, furniture, equipment (including computers), means of psychological testing, office supplies and other requirements, need to be planned to match the projected growth of the practice. For a new practice, the initial set-up of the physical location from which the practice is conducted will be included in this strategy.

Financial strategy

In relation to financial strategy, the details of your other strategies for business growth (marketing, service and resources) must be underpinned by a solid financial plan. This part of the business plan provides a link between all your other ideas for development of new services, conducting marketing campaigns, and obtaining resources. It answers questions relating to how much income you will earn through new business initiatives, how much it will cost you to generate this income, and the source of funds.

A financial strategy takes into account your practice's past performance and includes projections for the future. It may include all or some of the following concepts:

- financial history;
- capital investment estimates;
- profit and loss statements;
- cash flow projections;
- balance sheets.

Financial history covers trends in profit and loss in the last three to five years. Capital investment can be estimated by the shortfall between the expenditure and the income at the end of the first financial year. If some shortfall is predicted, it needs to be covered by capital expenditure. You need to identify the source of these funds in your financial strategy. For example, it could be a bank loan, in which case the interest costs should be built into the overall expenditure. If you plan to use your own savings as capital, it may be worthwhile calculating the expected rate of return on this investment, in order to compare it to an equivalent investment elsewhere.

The next section in this handbook, on financial planning, covers the other three of the above concepts in some detail, as they comprise fundamental tools of budgeting. Elsewhere in this work you will find outlines of the profit and loss statement, a sample balance sheet, and a sample cash flow statement. If you do nothing else, the most important part to include is a thorough cash-flow projection. This statement will show the predicted amount of cash you need to have in the bank at any one time in order to carry on the business.

Implementation plan

Once your strategies are finalized, the next chapter in the business plan should consist of a step-by-step action plan for each of these strategies. It may be helpful to remember that an effective action plan needs to:

- be expressed in specific terms;
- contain realistic statements of action;
- contain achievable time frames;
- identify the person responsible for each action point;
- define the measure of success.

Your plan needs to cover all the strategies outlined in the preceding subsection, and so it may be divided into four parts (marketing, the service, resources, and finance). You will probably find it most efficient to delegate to others as many steps of the plan as possible. It pays to seek out people who are capable of ensuring high-quality outcomes with minimum supervision. For example, you may develop an ongoing relationship with a desktop publisher or graphic designer who will take most of the responsibility for the printing of your marketing materials and stationery. Your time, efficiently spent with them, will be most productive.

Your implementation plan is likely to be most effective when you incorporate it into your everyday diary planning, and in this way you continue to monitor its implementation. When deadlines are missed you can then readjust the plan, but keep in mind that any readjustment will have a flow-on effect on your financial planning. If, for example, your marketing material does not go out on time as estimated, the projected income from the targeted stream of clients is also unlikely to flow as quickly as expected. Thus you will need also to adjust the income and expenditure projections in the cash flow analysis.

Performance evaluation
Monitoring of the business plan should be performed on a regular basis. In practice, this will only occur when you recognize its potential power to help you in the development of your practice as a business in a systematic and stress-free manner. There is room in the business plan itself for stating how you will monitor the implementation of your action plans and strategies and how you will evaluate it. That is how you will measure its success at the end of a specified period of time.

The business plan needs to be flexible and it may need to be adjusted to respond to new opportunities and threats. While it is recommended that your implementation action plan, along with your cash-flow analysis, is monitored and adjusted on a monthly basis, it is normally accepted that the entire business plan should be redeveloped once a year.

If your practice consists of other staff, it is important to involve them in the process of business planning. Their involvement will ensure their commitment to growing the business along with you. Since they are part of your business, they can provide valuable input to identifying new opportunities for improvement. It is often easy to underestimate the wealth of knowledge that your staff – especially those in the reception area or general office – have about your clients. Involving your staff will also recognize their significance, with consequent improvement in morale.

3.5.4 *Where to get help*

The process of business planning should not overwhelm you. If your practice is small, you may choose to borrow some of the ideas from the above discussion and then follow your intuition. There is no doubt that a systematic and professional approach to running a practice calls for some high-level planning. There are also, of course, many experienced and skilful professionals who can assist you in this process.

You may approach a business adviser directly, but it is helpful to keep your accountant involved in all major developments in your practice. There are also some government-assisted, as well as sponsored, small-business assistance initiatives that provide free or low-cost advice and publications on business planning. A list of useful addresses is given in Appendix B.

3.6 Financial planning

The discussion of business planning covered the development of financial strategy in general terms. Financial planning in any business is an ongoing process that must be undertaken with commitment if you are serious about succeeding. Attention is drawn not only to the material set out below but, once again, to the extremely useful business starter kits available from the major banks.

3.6.1 Start-up costs

One way of looking at start-up costs is to make an estimate to determine the minimum amount required to start the practice. A reverse way is to estimate how much you can raise and then see if a practice can be started using that amount. Suppose you were to decide that £10,000 is the maximum available, then the question you would ask is, 'What can be achieved for that amount?' If the financial resources were very limited you would need to carefully itemize the start-up requirements.

The highest priority initial costs – those without which it would be difficult to start at all – are the 'non-reducibles' such as premises, professional indemnity insurance, accounting and legal services, telephone systems, marketing, printing of stationery and psychological tests. The amounts you spend on the last three of these can vary depending on the available funds. To this list you need to add a requirement for adequate income to support you while the practice gets going. Premises are a significant cost, but renting rooms with established clinics or using serviced offices will obviate the purchase of such things as furniture, photocopier, fax, cleaning and so forth. Although you will pay rent in such circumstances, it can be on a start-up basis of one session per week.

Psychologists can sometimes find suitable rooms owned by a specialist (say) who has agreed to lease them for the times when he or she is not using them. This often arises without advertisement, and the specialist is normally happy to have extra income for his down-time as a bonus. With careful selection of such premises, there might be the added advantage of gaining a good reputation with the specialist – and therefore referrals.

In the initial set-up of your practice, you may find it useful to prepare a separate list of items to be purchased and include the totals in the expenditure categories in your cash-flow projection. A sample list of the items you may consider when estimating your initial outlay is given in Appendix C. An alternative way to purchasing the equipment and furniture for cash is leasing from a finance company. Your accountant should be able to advise you on the best lease arrangements or introduce you to a lease broker who can get acceptable interest rates for you. If you prefer to do-it-yourself, you can approach banks or other financial institutions and discuss with them their commercial leasing arrangements.

One particular advantage of leasing equipment is that you do not have to outlay a large sum of money up front, and instead make regular payments that can be met out of generated income each month. The other important advantage of leasing is that it is tax-deductible. On the other hand, the disadvantage is the higher cost of interest that makes the equipment you purchase more expensive, especially since you usually cannot obtain leases for second-hand equipment.

If cost-efficiency is your priority, it is possible to locate good-value equipment at various office furniture and equipment auctions, or at second-hand stores. As you do so, you need to bear in mind the cost of your time being expended on searching for bargains. Every hour you spend away from your practice you cannot earn income; thus you must take into account the cost of lost opportunity of earning when deciding on how to finance your initial set-up. To balance such a purely economic and rational view of the world, it is conceivable that you make a considered choice to spend more of your time in the initial stages of your business on setting it up rather than earning.

In order to undertake a more in-depth analysis of your expenditure, you may choose to group it into 'fixed' and 'variable' cost categories. 'Fixed' costs are such items as rent, utilities, and wages, which cannot generally be avoided whatever the level of business being undertaken. If there is a need to adjust or reduce expenditure, the 'variable' costs (such as the purchase of psychometric tests) are easier to reduce and should be targeted first. At the same time it is easier to estimate budgets when more of the costs are fixed, and so whenever possible you may consider alternative ways of funding items that attract variable costs.

The attitude to the start-up sum is critical here. Many small businesses fail – and many of those fail through undercapitalization. Others fail for want of investment in time and enterprise. The balance to be maintained is between firm containment of expenses and appropriate investment of money. Without firm budgetary control, whatever sum there is soon gets frittered away: but without imaginative investment on significant issues (such as marketing initiatives) the practice will never succeed. To this end, the cash-flow analysis becomes crucial.

3.6.2 Ongoing costs

A guide to ongoing costs is provided in Table 3.3 (see page 49), which is a sample cash-flow projection that is explained in detail in a later section. The list of possible expenditures includes (but is not limited to) bank charges, cleaning costs, light and power, National Insurance contributions, postage, pension costs and VAT. See Table 3.3 for a fuller list.

3.6.3 *Financial budgeting and analysis*

Although the financial standing of the business is the ultimate measure of its viability, this point is often denied or rationalized away by business owners. Unless your practice is able to earn sufficient income to provide adequate remuneration for yourself and your staff, as well as to pay your suppliers on time, you would be better to earn income in paid employment.

Psychologists, along with other professionals working in human services, are in most cases inadequately prepared for the financial management demands of a business. Because it is far easier to spend time on the activities we like best and avoid those we like least, financial plans are usually not given the attention they deserve. After all, they will provide the final evidence for your decision to proceed with the set-up or otherwise of your private practice. The objective of financial planning is to estimate accurately how much your business activities (which are contained in your business plan's marketing and resources strategies) are going to cost; and how much revenue can be generated from selling the products (as defined by your business plan's service strategy).

If you are preparing a budget after having been in practice for some time, you will be able to base your predictions on existing figures, and estimate those related to the new ideas, expansions, or marketing campaigns. If this is your first attempt at planning your finances, you must be prepared for some serious guesswork. At the same time, you should be as realistic as possible, both about your ability to win new clients (that is, earn income) and about the level of expenditure necessary to run the business. It is far better to be conservative when estimating your financial situation, and adjust it on a regular basis as more information about your performance becomes available, than to be over-optimistic.

The basic financial tools for performing financial budgeting and analysis are, once again, the balance sheet, the profit and loss statement, and the cash-flow projections, each of which is described in more detail after the matter of taxation has been discussed.

3.6.4 *Taxation*

The handling of taxation matters is a significant consideration. One issue is the need to ensure that PAYE is deducted and forwarded for all employees; another is the payment of personal income tax; a third is compliance with VAT requirements (noting that private psychology practice is *not* VAT-exempt). The deduction and forwarding of National Insurance payments is yet another obligation placed on employers.

Self-employed people pay what is termed 'Class 2' contributions, and may qualify for a 'small earnings exemption' if net income is low. Where there are employees, one has a responsibility to ensure that making appropriate payments protects the employees. Provided that the annual turnover does not exceed a certain sum, it is not necessary to register for VAT. If one does, however, the input and output taxes may be balanced.

There is a useful guide to the VAT issue in the British Psychological Society pamphlet *Private Practice as a Psychologist* (1996, pp. 12–16). It is worth emphasizing that observing taxation regulations is not only a legal requirement and a civil duty but also an issue that, if not observed properly, carries the capacity to become a problem of the first magnitude. If one does not abide by one's obligations, there is the prospect that audits and claims for unpaid tax could wreck a practice – and possibly a professional reputation. As always in financial matters, expert advice is crucial.

Income tax is payable on profit. Other income and allowances make up the liability for income tax. Unused capital allowances may be moved forward to offset future profits, but unused personal allowances have no such advantage. Those working in a limited liability company must pay PAYE tax – whether they be owners, directors or simply employees. The profit of a company is also subject to corporation tax.

3.6.5 *The balance sheet*

The balance sheet is a commonly accepted term but it is not well understood. In fact, most people tend to refer to a balance sheet in their everyday conversation when they really mean a profit and loss statement, which is a far easier concept to comprehend.

A balance sheet is a table of your practice's (or any business's) total worth – a list of all your assets and liabilities. It is essentially a tool of economists and accountants for appraising the well-being of a company at a particular time. Although it is a vital piece of paper to them, it will probably never excite a psychologist – even one in private practice. Unlike other tools, the balance sheet is also less functional for budgeting and financial planning. Nevertheless, it is worthwhile to understand the terms contained within the balance sheet because they will make a significant impact on your practice. When you are ready to sell the business, its value will be expressed in the balance sheet.

Table 3.1: A sample balance sheet

Balance sheet for the financial year: 1/4/2001 to 31/3/2002

FIXED ASSETS:
Land and buildings £
Motor vehicles £

CURRENT ASSETS:
Short-term deposits £
Trade debtors (people owing money to you) £
less provisions for doubtful debts (£)
Cash in Hand £
Cash at Bank £
Prepaid insurances £

INTANGIBLE ASSETS:
Formation expenses £
Patents £

INVESTMENTS:
Shares £
Deposits £

TOTAL £

LONG-TERM LIABILITIES:
Mortgage £
Other loans £

CURRENT LIABILITIES:
Bank overdraft £
Trade creditors (people you owe money to) £
Provisions (e.g. for taxation) £

CAPITAL:
Issued capital (if company) £
Directors' loans £
Retained earnings (profits you left in company) £

TOTAL £

You may find it worthwhile to gain more insight from accounting books for novices. Table 3.1 shows a sample balance sheet. It is divided into two main parts: liabilities and assets. The liabilities are essentially funds you owe, and the assets are the things you own. The two sides are always in balance, hence its name.

The liabilities include:

- long-term liabilities: all loans, such as mortgages, that are long term in nature;
- current liabilities: all debt that you need to repay in the short term – for example, a bank overdraft and all the bills that are due to be paid to suppliers;
- capital: all retained profits, and value of shares if your business structure is a company.

The assets include:

- fixed assets: assets of a long-term nature, such as buildings or motor vehicles (sometimes referred to as non-current assets);
- current assets: assets easily converted into cash, such as bank deposits and debts owed to you by your clients;
- intangible assets: assets that only have a value if the business is ongoing (such as goodwill), and others including those that consist of expenses incurred at initial set-up;
- investments: shares in other companies, and loans made to others.

Your practice's balance sheet will be prepared by your accountant once a year (or on a more regular basis if you so request) and will provide you with a 'snapshot' value of your net assets. The balance sheets from at least three years of business operation will be carefully scrutinized by a bank if you apply for a substantial bank loan, and so it is a good idea to understand the basics. You certainly do not need to know its intricacies to operate a successful and profitable practice. However, it will be hard to do so without the working knowledge of the next two financial tools outlined below.

3.6.6 The profit and loss statement

The second financial tool, the profit and loss statement, is probably the most intuitive to understand because it has an immediate impact on your hip pocket. A profit and loss statement consists of the net difference between income and expenditure. In its simplest form, it looks like the example shown in Table 3.2.

Table 3.2: A sample profit and loss statement

Profit and loss statement for the financial year 1/4/2001 to 31/3/2002

Income

Professional fees	£ _____
Royalties	£ _____
Courses / seminars	£ _____
Other income	£ _____
Total income	£ _____

Expenses

Wages and salaries	£ _____
Premises	£ _____
Insurances etc.	£ _____
Other expenses	£ _____
Total expenses	less £ _____

Gross profit (loss) £ _____

Tax less £ _____

Net profit (loss) £ _____

3.6.7 Cash-flow projections

Profit and loss statements for past years can be presented, along with projections for the next three to five years, to demonstrate the trend in profits (or losses). To make this sort of projection useful for yourself and not just the bank manager and accountant, you need to estimate income and expenditure in a more detailed manner. In your first year's budget, for example, you need to calculate the entire costs of initial set-up to ensure you have enough cash to purchase all vital equipment and carefully evaluate various options such as renting rooms, purchasing second-hand or new furniture, etc.

The most powerful tool for performing this sort of detailed financial analysis is a cash-flow projection – your third financial tool. Cash-flow projection is a table showing an estimate of how much ready cash you will collect and spend each month. No matter how big or how small your practice, whether this is your first business plan or whether your practice has been operating for years, once you discover the power of thorough cash-flow analysis your capability to run private practice (or any business, for that matter) will greatly increase.

If you attend to nothing else in this section, and even if you ignore the intricacies of the business plan altogether, it is recommended that

Table 3.3: A sample cash-flow projection

For the period April–June 2001   Date prepared: 26/02/01

	April		May		June	
	Actual (£)	Est. (£)	Actual (£)	Est. (£)	Actual (£)	Est. (£)
INCOME (SOURCE)						
Seminars						
Compensation clients						
Private clients						
Sub-total						
Royalties						
Other income						
TOTAL						
EXPENDITURE						
Accounting fees						
Advertising / marketing						
Bank charges						
Cleaning						
Computer software						
Courier						
Employee amenities						
Employer liability insurance						
Entertainment						
Heating						
Insurance						
Leases						
Legal fees						
Library						
Light and power						
National Insurance						
Office equipment						
Office security						
Pension costs						
Postage						
Printing						
Rates						
Rent for office						
Repairs and maintenance						
Stationery						
Telephone						
Training						
Travel and accommodation						
V.A.T.						
Vehicle expenses						
Wages and tax						
TOTAL						
SURPLUS(DEFICIT)						
Bank balance						

you at least consider the simple yet essential tool of financial planning, described below. The reason for such confidence in cash-flow analyses is that it takes a lot of the uncertainty and anxiety out of business planning. If done in sufficient detail, and with a realistic and conservative approach, you can predict where the income will come from and how much cash you need in the bank, month by month. No more sleepless nights!

By this means, all transactions are documented and an analysis can be adjusted each time new information becomes available about how much money you really have spent. Your practical knowledge of computer spreadsheets will make this exercise much more efficient, but it is no embarrassment to use a large piece of paper (preferably with pre-printed financial columns) and a pocket calculator. The structure of a cash-flow projection is not unlike the profit and loss statement, except that income and expenditure are broken down into much more detailed categories, and the figures are estimated for each month. The example in Table 3.3 shows a period covering three months, but it is most common to prepare such a table for a 12-month period.

Another useful feature that should be built into the cash-flow projection is the running figure for each month, alongside your previous estimates. This provides ongoing feedback to you about the accuracy of your projections, and allows for adjustment of the next month's estimated figures. This monthly adjustment depends on your ongoing monitoring of all expenses and income, and on taking time to check how your business is performing, at least on a monthly basis. It also depends on the financial data available to you.

Your receipts, invoices and cheque stubs must be organized in a systematic manner so that a monthly financial check will not be a difficult and time-consuming task. The information systems that are vital for this process are further discussed in detail in the section on information systems. You may choose, of course, to pass this task on to your bookkeeper or accountant. If you do so, you must keep in mind that you are the only person who has the information about the direction in which your business is heading and your capacity to generate more income.

When estimating income (as set out in the top part of Table 3.3), you can split it into as many categories as you find useful; for example, each project or group of clients being referred from one particular source may constitute one type of income. In this way, you can reflect the expected income from (for instance) the planned marketing campaigns included in your marketing strategy. Similarly, the bottom part of the table consists of expenditure items, also divided into as many categories as seems appropriate to provide sufficient detail for planning. Ideally, these categories should correspond to the 'accounts' used by your accountant to analyse your final end-of-year profit and loss statement for taxation purposes. They can be even more detailed, however, so that the actual analysis immediately makes sense to you. For example, if you have a number of leases, you can separate each lease payment.

Remember that this table is to be a reflection of *actual* cash flow. That is, both income and expenditure should be entered in those months when cash is expected to come into the bank and payments are to be made. Some of the projects can last for an extended period of time, at the end of which you should issue an invoice for your services. The actual payment, however, may not appear until the terms of payment have expired, and in many cases much later (the issue of managing debt is further discussed elsewhere in this book). Conversely, when you receive bills from your suppliers you usually have a few weeks in which to pay. The payments and receipts of cash are entered in the cash-flow projection table in the month in which they are expected to be paid.

3.6.8 Obtaining a loan

It is possible to develop a successful psychology practice with very little capital investment, mainly because the business of psychology is neither stock- nor equipment-intensive. The success in what is sometimes colloquially referred to as 'brain business' has far more to do with the skills and capability of the practitioner than the amount of capital invested in marble offices and glossy brochures. At the same time, the often-committed error of most businesses is undercapitalization, that is, spending too little at the set-up stage and therefore reducing the potential future profit, which is linked to return on investment. To limit the initial capital outlay, most practitioners expend vast amounts of time instead of money – not an unreasonable approach in the absence of easily available funds.

It is likely, however, that at some stage of your practice's development you will recognize the need for funding for your plans in order to generate more business. The most accessible business funding is in the form of a bank overdraft. This usually requires some security, such as a mortgage over a family home, to the amount equal to the required overdraft. It is similar to a credit facility and not unlike a credit card, except that the amounts involved are as large as you can convince the bank manager you can safely repay.

This is where your business plan becomes essential. It is hard to portray a confident and businesslike image without a document that can demonstrate that you have seriously considered your business opportunities and prepared appropriate strategies. It is far better to present the plan at the first meeting with the bank manager. Your accountant will also advise you with respect to the availability of various funding options and their requirements. Although the business plan should be concise, it must include a financial analysis such as a cash-flow projection. You should not be surprised if a bank representative immediately turns to this section and works backwards from it, asking some pertinent questions about the validity of your optimism regarding the generation of income from clients about whom they have very little knowledge.

Once your line of credit is established, it is likely that your financial performance will be reviewed on a regular basis, which may involve forwarding your end-of-year financial statements and/or taxation returns to the lending bank. Most banks will charge you interest only when you use an overdraft facility, but there are some who still charge the establishment fee and ongoing fee for the privilege of having a line of credit whether you use it or not. It pays to do some shopping around to find the best deal, particularly with the competitive environment in the financial services sector that is prevalent nowadays.

As an alternative to bank overdrafts, you may consider short-term leasing or hire purchase arrangements. It is quite probable that most of the initial set-up funds will be needed for equipment, such as office furniture, computers, photocopier, or fax machine. As was mentioned earlier, and is repeated here for emphasis, as long as you are prepared to give personal guarantees and your credit history is not problematic, you will find it quite easy to make a lease arrangement, usually for three to five years, with some residual amount (e.g. 20–40 per cent) to be repaid at the end of the lease period. At that stage you may be ready to trade-in the old equipment anyway, and take out another lease.

Under a lease arrangement, the equipment remains the property of the finance company. Thus all the payments are tax-deductible. Under a hire purchase arrangement, you become the owner of the purchased goods, in which case they will appear as fixed assets in your balance sheet from the outset. Their depreciation as well as the interest paid to the financial institution are tax-deductible.

There are several sources of smaller funds to which the aspiring business starter might turn. These include private investors, building societies, finance houses, mortgaging the family home, and grants from governmental or business-subsidy sources. For the more ambitious and larger enterprises there are finance houses, merchant banks, and venture capital suppliers.

3.6.9 Wealth creation

While you are planning the financial aspects of your business, it is easy to forget that you should also be planning *your own* financial future. You are an independent entity from your business, although it may sometimes be difficult to separate the two. The initial 'honeymoon' period of private practice often gives way to a desire to 'have something to show for all my hard work' other than overdrafts, loans and a tired family. To prevent such physical, emotional and professional exhaustion, it is suggested that you consider your own financial future and view your business venture as part of your personal wealth creation and a path to financial independence.

Rather than viewing your practice as something that drives you, perhaps a healthier approach might be to use it as a tool to achieve your personal goals. Start with your own goals and personal mission – a topic of many worthwhile books (Covey, 1993). Once you have these clearly worked out in your mind or on paper, you will know the level of finances required. The structure and financial plan of your business should reflect those goals. For example, if your needs for ready cash are mainly long term, you will be wise to plan for substantial pension contributions as part of your own wealth creation. Although constantly changing, the personal pension system is still one of the most tax-effective ways to save for the future. You might even consider starting your own pension fund, with some assistance from your accountant and financial adviser, which can then provide your practice with funds to purchase equipment and/or building.

It will be appreciated that having a private practice or a business is rarely an end in itself but is, rather, a significant part of a larger life picture. Among the functions of a private practice are: the creation of an income; the development of a worthwhile economic asset; the development of a lifestyle that gives considerable autonomy; and an involvement in an enterprise that you regard as significantly worthwhile. Within that context, the financial and aspirational aspects are intertwined. Having a successful business not only keeps you financially successful and gives a sense of worth, but it also develops as something that you own and can eventually sell if you wish. Part of your planning may be to develop a business that you can sell to do something different, or use the proceeds to eventually retire.

During the course of your career, you may come to derive benefits that were not foreseen. For example, what you do may be so innovative as to result in the development of a psychological test for which you own the copyright. Other benefits may be to develop a course that you can franchise, to write a book that significantly enhances your professional reputation, to franchise your practice, or to provide a unique service.

Late in his life, in 1952, the novelist A.J. Cronin wrote a book called *Adventures in Two Worlds*. The general thrust of what he had to say is that in one's youth the material and the technological hold sway. As one gets older, the intangible world of values becomes progressively more dominant. These two worlds are, in other words, of different salience at different times of life. A business must be financially successful if it is to be regarded as successful overall – but not financially successful at any price. Thus the intangibles become increasingly important as your career progresses. Late in a career, few would want to reflect that they have become successful by trampling on others, and by shady behaviour.

The goodwill that an ethical practice demonstrates is convertible to cash on sale. Attention to cash flow, and attention to wealth creation by innovation and hard work, go hand in hand with close attention to professional values. In a rural community, for instance, your plan may be to make available a service formerly denied those living in remoter communities. It is this use of creative intelligence, combined with hard work, that makes really successful enterprises. To succeed at a higher level, there is a need to work smarter rather than harder. Here the solution is to indulge in some creative thinking, often helped by an interchange of ideas with a creative and discreet colleague.

Your long-term personal aim should be building wealth; otherwise you may find that a lot of money has slipped through your hands over the many years you have been in private practice. Some helpful advice can be obtained from financial planners and investment specialists. Exercise caution, however, particularly when the advice given is not on a fee-for-service basis. When a financial planner gains income from a commission from certain investment funds, it is not hard to imagine which ones will be recommended. Always find out how the income of your adviser is derived.

3.6.10 Estate planning

Estate planning is even more long term and has to do with what happens after you have left the practice or have died. It is important to consider your will and the way your dependants will be looked after, as well as how your business will be managed in your absence. The need for a current will applies to anyone, but particularly to someone operating a business under a complex structure. Your will should be up to date and reviewed regularly to ensure that it reflects your intentions.

Consider establishing an Enduring Power of Attorney – which means that you will appoint another person to act on your behalf in financial and personal matters in a situation where you are unable to act for yourself, whether for geographical or medical reasons.

You may also consider a testamentary trust will, through which you can establish a discretionary trust for each of the beneficiaries in the will. The primary beneficiary then has a number of options for their share of the estate: for example, the person could take all or part of the capital immediately or at any time during the remainder of their life;

the person could distribute income from year to year to relatives of their choice; or they could take a capital loan from the trust without interest.

Some trusts provide for pension entitlements. When creating your will, you must consider who will control the business in the future: how you would like the management succession to take place, and what roles should various people play in your absence? It makes sense, of course, to talk to these persons first about your plans. It is always advisable to seek professional assistance when you are unsure of what to do, and in this case your solicitor should be consulted.

4

Establishing your practice

So far, you will have completed a soul-searching exercise as to whether you are ready to enter the business world, chosen the area of your practice, and prepared a business plan. The time has now come to begin the practice. You will need to make some basic decisions about such things as the physical setting and your stationery. Think of yourself as a project manager, or a coordinator of numerous set-up activities such as printing, selecting equipment, identifying options for a telephone system, negotiating with insurance salespeople, and the like.

If you are the sort of person who dislikes this sort of administrative activity, it might be better to seek someone's assistance. Since you are the one who will be the principal behind the practice, it will pay to spend some time on these mundane issues and work through the pain. This stage will pass as you become established, most of the decisions are made, and the many tasks undertaken, and they will not have to be faced again.

As you upgrade your telephone or computer systems, increase your premises, review your stationery and so on, you will be able to enhance the practice and correct some of the errors made in the initial set-up stage. Your becoming business 'street wise' at this early stage will have many advantages in the future.

4.1 Choosing your practice name

If the business structure that you have chosen is a sole operator using your own name, this decision will be simple. It may be of interest to note that even though your business name or company name has been selected, this structure can still trade under another name that is more appropriate for the marketplace. An example is ABC-XYZ Nominees Pty Ltd trading as People Professionals, where the trading name is displayed more prominently. If you would like to choose this option, you will need to register the trading name with the appropriate body, as you would with any other business name.

In selecting the name of your practice, the guiding thought should be the perception of your target market. Besides giving *you* a sense of identity, it must also send an effective message to those with whom you want to do business. For example, if your target group consists of lawyers, it will be worthwhile to design the sort of name that communicates a sense of prestige and credibility, not unlike a name associated with a solicitors' firm; for example, Menzies and Associates. If your selected market comprises chief executives of large companies, your practice name should convey a corporate image; for example, IPC Corporate Solutions. One way to identify a suitable name is to search through the currently registered names or even the relevant section of *Yellow Pages*: Training and Development, Psychologists, Management Consultants, and such like. You will discover, for example, that names of many corporations tend to consist of three-letter acronyms, such as IBM, BMW, RAC – or some other euphonious combination such as KPMG or BT.

To check whether your perception matches that of your target-market grouping, it is recommended that you perform a 'pilot test' on the name and what it conveys using a selected yet representative sample. Here is another instance of where you can put your hard-earned psychological research skills to good use – they will give you a competitive advantage over businesses managed by people without such skills. The idea of pilot testing is applicable to any other activities involving communication with a target audience – for example, in marketing.

Although it is easy to expend a lot of effort, time and money on selecting the name and testing its acceptance in the marketplace, this task should be seen in its proper perspective. Your practice name is important in that it immediately communicates a message; the service you provide and how you provide it will, in many instances, overshadow any effect of the name. There are many stories of psychologists – and other professionals in private practice – who had hired business-name and design experts, only to end up with a name like [Surname] Psychology Services or [Surname] Corporate Psychology.

4.2 Designing and using a logo

Following the decision on the practice name, the dilemma of designing an appropriate logo for the business usually appears, calling for some creative flair. As with the selection of the name, there is a danger of investing a disproportionate amount of time and resources into this task. It is best to commence the process with a clear list of descriptors and characteristics of your practice. You may, for example, describe your business in terms of feelings you would like to generate in the person dealing with you. Should it have a corporate image, or a 'soft and warm' feeling? What sort of first impression would you like to create in someone who looks at your logo?

Many companies take their business logo very seriously because it identifies their public image. Sometimes they change it in line with a *new* public image they would like to create. Such public changes have been recently observed in which it is interesting to note that, after much discussion and design creation, quite simple images appear (example: BP-Amoco in 2000, with its green-and-yellow 'sunflower' motif). There is a lesson to be learnt here from observing others go through the process of logo design, namely that the simpler and clearer the image the better. It does not matter if it is abstract, since everyone will use their own 'ink blot test' to interpret it. If it produces the sort of meaning and image you would like to create in your audience, it has fulfilled its purpose. To prevent others utilizing it, you may register your business logo as a patent or trademark. Your solicitor will advise you on the process and cost involved.

The British Psychological Society has a logo that may be used under certain designated conditions. There is a Society memorandum dated 24 May 1999 expressing the serious nature of the use of the logo. This alerts us to the difficulties that might arise when the Society is engaged with another organization. It is clear from that document that the use of the logo must be under the control of the Society, and so members are strongly advised to consult the Society before engaging in any form of use of the logo. Attention is also drawn to the following British Psychological Society statement: 'Since the Society's "Psyche Logo" is not available for use by individual members, the Board of Directors has authorised Chartered Psychologists to use a specially prepared logo for business and advertising purposes'.

4.3 Designing and printing stationery

Once your practice has a name, and possibly a logo, it has its identity. The next step is to demonstrate its identity to the world around you. This is first done by printing business stationery, which includes business cards, letterheads, envelopes, 'with compliments' slips and fax headers.

4.3.1 Business cards

The normally accepted custom is that you authenticate your identity through your business card. The business card communicates your status within the business entity, as well as your professional standing. It is suggested that a business card contain:

- business trading name and logo, if applicable;
- your full name;
- your title within the business entity (e.g., consultant, counselling psychologist);
- your qualifications;
- business address;
- telephone numbers on which you would like your clients to contact you (e.g., business, mobile, home);
- fax number;
- pager number;
- email address;
- website address (if appropriate).

If your practice involves making appointments with clients, you may consider including text on the reverse side of your business card, providing space for time of the next appointment. For example, 'Your next appointment is: Date: _____ Time: _____'.

It is your responsibility to make sure that you are legally permitted to use the title and identification that you include on all stationery, including your business card. Only if you are a Chartered Psychologist may you call yourself one. The claim to specialization is subject to the cautions mentioned elsewhere in this book.

In offices where a number of professionals practise, you will usually find small display stands containing all the relevant business cards. You may consider placing your cards on the reception counter so that your clients reporting to reception, or any other potential clients, can take one.

Some practitioners have chosen to design and print their own stationery, given the easy and relatively inexpensive access to desktop publishing software, a computer and high-quality printers such as laser printers. A word of warning here: although it is possible to design a relatively high-quality letterhead and print it directly via a laser printer with each letter or invoice, this is not the case with a business card. One reason for this is the thickness of the paper stock on which business cards are normally printed; a laser printer cannot normally handle that thickness. Second, you will need to cut printed paper into the required number of cards, making straight edges with even margins rather difficult to achieve, even with a paper guillotine. The resultant image left with the client is that the business is not able to afford 'real' business cards. While producing one's own cards may be quite appropriate for a business involved in the creative arts, such as pottery or calligraphy, it is not the norm among professional service providers and tends to be a false economy.

4.3.2 *Business letterheads*

Along with the business card, you will also need to design a matching letterhead so that your practice can establish an official contact with the outside world through letters, invoices and reports. If your practice is trading under an incorporated structure, such as a limited company or a trustee company, there are special legal requirements for displaying on the letterhead: the business trading name (if different from the full name of the company) the full name of the company including 'plc', 'Limited' or 'Ltd' as appropriate, and the company's registered number (a unique number that identifies your company).

In addition to these legal requirements, you will also wish to include on your letterhead:

- practice address (or addresses, if there are more than one – in which case you may like to indicate to which address correspondence should be addressed);
- telephone number, usually the main office/clinic contact;
- facsimile (fax) number;
- email address.

If your practice trades under a registered business name, the name and the registered business number must be displayed on letterheads, invoices, receipts, written orders, and written demands for payment. You may wish to print invoice stationery, which specifically includes the invoice-related details. It is acceptable within the professional-service business world to use your letterheads for this purpose, with the added word 'Invoice' prominently placed somewhere on the page.

It is possible to produce letterheads of reasonable quality using home/office computer technology. Your scanned logo, together with your practice's name, address and telephone numbers, can be printed from a template every time the contents of a letter or report are produced. This assumes the use of either a laser or, at least, an ink-jet printer. The advantage of such a course of action is that you do not have to spend extra on large numbers of preprinted letterheads.

The disadvantages of printing one's own letterheads are the loss of quality, a possible limitation to black print, and the need to print every time you want to use a letterhead, even for handwritten material. While this approach may be quite reasonable for invoices, you need to consider again the sort of image you would like your private practice to project into its market. If your recognized value is to be low cost and self-sufficient, this would be an effective way of demonstrating your commitment to such values. Such an approach may well be appropriate for low-income clients or community non-profit organizations, but it may not be a desirable message in the corporate sector.

The reason for higher expectations of printed quality is that personal computers have raised the standards for everyone. This means that a secondary-school student is able to produce a good-quality report quite cheaply. The corporate world, at the same time, because of its competitive paradigm, needs to distinguish between its different levels of commitment to quality.

In addition to the quality of print, your image will also be projected through the stock on which your letterhead is printed: its thickness and type, the number of colours used and the overall design. While it is important to reiterate that there is far more to running a successful practice than image creation, it pays to be mindful of the perceptions generated in the client via symbols embedded into the business and professional service culture. If funds are your foremost consideration, the cost of the stationery design can well be minimized without greatly compromising your practice standing. As you consider investing more money into the business, you may give thought to all the seemingly small impressions (such as stationery) that can yield big impacts.

4.3.3 Envelopes

It is standard to display your private practice name, logo and postal address on the outside of an envelope, usually on the left-hand top corner. The address you choose to place on the envelope should be your preferred postal address. If you practise from a number of clinics or offices, this address will correspond to the one from which your practice is being administered. If you have a post office box, or a special postal bag arrangement, you may choose to limit this information to the postal address. Telephone numbers do not normally appear on envelopes.

4.3.4 Compliments slips

Compliments slips are pieces of paper – usually one-third of an A4 page in size, or even smaller – to use when enclosing material in a package 'with compliments'. Such slips are attached to items that are being transmitted via post or courier, and they usually contain short handwritten messages or a signature. Often, the slips are simply attached to a relevant document to signify its origin, without any writing.

As well as the eponymous two words, compliments slips should contain your practice name, logo, address and contact details. If the resources which you have earmarked for spending on stationery design and printing are very limited, the compliments slips can be omitted and your letterhead used instead for those infrequent occasions when a handwritten note is necessary.

4.3.5 Fax headers

If you plan to use a facsimile machine, you will find it useful to design a fax header sheet, which identifies you and the recipient, and for typing or hand-writing a message to the recipient. Fax header sheets are used as the first page of an outgoing fax to easily identify both the sender and the recipient.

Give some thought to the design of your sheet to enable it to be easily identified with your practice, particularly if you use fax communication on a frequent basis. It should include at least:

- your name;
- the practice name, address, phone and fax numbers;
- the number of pages being transmitted (clearly stating whether the header sheet is included in the total count);
- the recipient's name, phone and fax numbers;
- email address.

Because the process of faxing drastically reduces the quality of anything transmitted, there is little point in obtaining high-quality fax headers through a commercial printers. Computer printing in this instance is quite satisfactory. Indeed, some computer-based fax software provides facilities for the design and transmission of appropriate header sheets.

4.4 Choosing the practice site

4.4.1 What's in an address?

The above discussion of printing stationery has introduced the notion of an image of private practice, its projection and importance. It is probably true to say that anything a business does in its communication with the public, and therefore with its clients, contributes to its overall image. The message of the business's values is communicated at times very subtly, and often more powerfully than a business owner is prepared to admit. One of those not-so-subtle messages is embedded within the practice address.

The authors' anecdotal evidence suggests that when unsolicited material arrives on a potential client's or referrer's desk, the first question tends to be: 'Do I know this person or this company?' If the answer is 'No', and your material still has the reader's interest, their next quick check is the address. The type of address that has the least trust and attraction is a post office box number, without a street address.

As the venue from which your private practice operates sends a powerful message about yourself, your values and your status as a provider of professional services, it is recommended that you choose wisely. If financial imperatives prevent you from renting professional premises on a full-time basis, you may consider a sessional basis, or a staged process of beginning at home and moving when client referrals or projects increase to sufficiently high levels.

4.4.2 *The joys and pitfalls of a home-based practice*

While some counselling and clinical psychologists currently operate their practices from home, the appropriateness of home as a counselling clinic has been questioned for decades. The arguments against using your home centre upon the undermining of the professional image of psychology, and the safety risk to which all household occupants are exposed. The lone, home-based practitioner is marginally more vulnerable to violence, and to accusations of compromising behaviour.

Another important consideration appears to be that relating to the issue of professionalism in psychology. In recent years more small businesses operate from home than ever before because of the progress in computer and telecommunications technology. This change has not been observed among professionals dealing with the public in relationships essentially based on professional trust. Thus, there are relatively few medical practitioners or lawyers practising from home.

The most important factor to consider in choosing the location for your practice is the effect it will have on the potential and existing clients. It may be, for example, quite appropriate for an educational psychologist to provide a service for students at home, as they are likely to expect a similar locale for other professionals servicing them – for example, music teachers. Organizational clients, on the other hand, will expect that their employees will be hosted in a professional office when they are referred for a selection assessment. You will get most attention from readers of your brochures if you are in a well-recognized area, such as a recognized business district of a town or city, or an inner suburb with an established name for medical or business offices.

Clients seeking personal psychological assistance will probably accept a home-based clinic without complaining unless their expectations have been previously heightened by other professional clinic standards. Even then, because of the nature of the relationship, they are unlikely to express their surprise at, or dissatisfaction with, the quality of the premises of their psychologist.

It is important also to consider that the fees you charge are linked to your client's perception of the intrinsic value of your services. Thus, if you practise from a suburban home–office, it would normally be expected that your practice's savings on commercial office rent would be reflected in your fees. In some countries, the move to 'small office home office' (SOHO) is becoming popular. Its essence is the integration of communication systems, the provision of a complete range of office needs, and advice about how they might be most efficiently used. It needs to be remembered that such home-based businesses are rarely operating as professional or consulting rooms dealing with the public, but those systems have much to teach the prospective private practitioner.

In the light of such trends in the British workscape, it should be noted that it might be quite appropriate for some professionals to operate a successful private practice from home. An example could be an organizational psychologist, most of whose work is conducted on the client's premises or at hired training venues. In a situation where financial resources are limited, quite a valid decision may be to save on office lease costs and invest instead in technology such as computers, software, or presentation tools. The gains from such investments are likely to outweigh the disadvantages associated with working from home, at least in the short term.

There are further advantages of working from home. One of the more obvious ones is reduced travel time, as long as this saving in time is spent on other productive activities. Proximity to your cohabitants and the flexibility of being able to engage in home activities while you are not involved in practice work can be both positive and negative, depending on your personal situation. A financial advantage is that you may be able to offset the increased costs of electricity, heating and telephone against the business. If you are planning to do so for an extended period of time, you will need to seek advice from your accountant.

There may, however, be capital gains tax implications if your home is used for income-earning purposes, and for when you plan to sell it. If you only claim consumables (a suitable proportion of heating, light, phone, etc.), it should not affect the taxation position of your family home when you come to sell it. If you start costing the premises, seek an accountant's advice. At the same time, you will need to weigh up the disadvantage associated with isolation when working on your own at home.

4.4.3 Sharing professional rooms

There are a number of alternatives for the practice location – other than your own home – that are economical and offer a more professional image. As previously mentioned, one of these is sharing a clinic or office with another professional. Such an arrangement can be either on a sessional basis or for an agreed regular period. 'Sessional' means that you only pay for the rooms when you actually use them, usually when you see a client or need to use facilities for other reasons. The other payment basis involves a regular rent per week or month, for an agreed number of days, irrespective of whether or not you use the office. While the former option is usually more expensive per hour, it may be more cost-effective if the number of clients you see is low and unpredictable.

It is worth repeating that the type of professionals with whom you could share a room will depend on the area of psychology in which you specialize. It is expected that the premises will in some way resemble the type that your clientele will find attractive and appropriate. If you do not have any personal helpful contacts and cannot locate relevant advertisements in the local papers, you may choose simply to call in and introduce yourself to the owner. You may find that such professionals are keen to negotiate a rental deal to mutual satisfaction, especially when they have one or more rooms vacant on their property.

One advantage of such an arrangement with an established office or clinic is that there are usually staffed reception areas, whose services can also be negotiated as part of the overall rental. This becomes one of the most significant issues when attempting to operate a practice, initially with no full-time staff to manage the incoming calls – a fundamental activity for a business constantly dealing with people and appointments.

Depending on the extent of the reception and administrative assistance you receive at the shared premises, it can be referred to as a version of a 'serviced office' arrangement. Thus, when working out how much is reasonable for accommodation, you need to take into account all the costs of the reception, salaries, communication systems and telephones. Once you know how much this would cost you if you were to set up you own premises, you might then be willing to pay more when renting premises with extra reception facilities. Furthermore, you will also have a basis on which to argue that the rental is too expensive.

4.4.4 Renting serviced offices

Serviced offices are becoming increasingly available in major cities, in response to a greater number of consulting professionals of all kinds who practise on their own. The target clients for such service businesses are those professionals who recognise the need for a better address than a home office, and who cannot afford full-time staff to fulfil their administrative needs.

As was mentioned earlier, in a serviced-office arrangement you rent one or more fully furnished rooms for an agreed amount and utilize all the available facilities at an extra charge on a user-pays basis. This usually includes use of a boardroom, typing facilities, facsimile and photocopying machines, and a computer. You have an allocated telephone number and it is answered in your practice name, as per agreed instructions. Your telephone messages and your mail are also stored for you, and other normal administrative support is provided.

Serviced offices vary from highest-quality office buildings in the central business district of a large city through to smaller places in outer suburbs. Advertisements for such premises can usually be found in newspapers since the turnover of their clients is relatively high. Some serviced offices provide a very low-priced entry into such an arrangement, giving the right to the address on your letterhead, your telephone answered in your practice's name, a basic mail-holding facility, and occasional (and paid) use of an office. Their understandable commercial aim is to increase usage, with the expectation that your business will grow and need more rental time.

The more reputable serviced office providers usually have reciprocal arrangements in the major cities in which they have no presence. This means that if you rent an office in one city, you have a right to use similar offices in other cities. In some cases you may use all of their other-city addresses on your letterhead. This option will most likely appeal to an organizational or vocational psychologist who needs to portray an appropriate image to corporate clients; counselling and clinical psychologists need to ensure that their clients' calls are dealt with appropriately, generally by making appointments, and so this arrangement is less likely via a serviced office reception. If it does occur in the latter case, however, and given that the serviced office reception personnel have as their main role the taking of messages for you to return calls, some staff training may be necessary.

4.4.5 Leasing independent office space

Another practice location option is to lease independent office space. You need to be ready to make this move as far as your business development plan is concerned because it will have obvious risks attached. First, the immediate rental cost and the ongoing nature of your liability for such payments have to be considered. The lease period usually lasts for a minimum of two years. Lease contracts generally include penalties if you wish to cancel before the expiry date, at least to cover the landlord's cost of finding another tenant. For this and other reasons it is recommended that you seek the advice of your solicitor before signing any contract – as you should with any binding legal agreement. Minimize your risks, and make yourself fully aware of all the implications of your decision.

Additional costs in the initial outlay, which are associated with renting your premises, include their full furnishing and partitioning (unless such fitting-out has already been done). Although office partitioning can be costly, it is sometimes left behind by tenants as it is generally cheaper to build these again at a new location than to shift them. One of the distinguishing features of offices required by psychologists is the need for an enclosed area for each professional in order to create a confidential atmosphere. Thus, the required office space per practitioner is usually more than the equivalent for other offices for which open floor plan is adequate.

As a rough estimate, each single office requires a minimum of 14 square metres (150 square feet). When you add a reception, administration, waiting and kitchen area to your estimates, it is possible to operate a comfortable practice for one practitioner from around 47 square metres (500 square feet) – i.e., something like 8 metres by 6 metres. With more practitioners operating from the one location, requirements will not increase pro rata because of the shared reception, kitchen, etc.

The area you require is important because the rental prices are usually expressed in terms of cost per square unit (metre or foot) per annum. Hence, in newspaper advertisements (usually hidden in the 'Business' sections of daily papers, as opposed to the 'Properties' sections) you will often see a reference to 'office space', its area, and price with little further information. You obviously must know the prices, to provide a basis for the estimate of your expenditure. When you have this information, make sure that you know whether the quote is in pounds sterling per square metre per year or pounds per square foot per year.

The price will of course vary according to the quality and location of the building, and the overall current demand and supply ratios of office space in the particular city. In addition to the agreed rental amount, you can also expect to pay for 'outgoings', including rates, water, electricity, and other such utilities, which can add a few pounds per square unit per year to the overall cost. Parking can also add more costs to the equation, particularly if the office is in an identified business district. As a general rule, in estimating your budget and your ability to afford rented premises, their cost should not exceed a certain proportion of your practice's annual income – say, one-third at the very most.

When deciding on the option of practice premises, you need to take into account not just the current income but the projected income according to your service, marketing and financial strategies. You need to be guided to some extent by your vision of where you would like your business to be and what sort of clients you would like to service. Then your behaviour needs to reflect this vision, including where and how you receive your clients. Operating a business from leased offices will also call for independent staffing of at least the reception area. The person performing this function can also be responsible for administration of the practice.

4.4.6 *Owning an office building*

Another even more expensive option, in the short term, is owning your own building. When you account for all the rental costs over a number of years, it may occur to you that there are parallels with your rental or ownership of a residential property. Most people opt for purchasing their home, for instance, because of the long-term gains, and this might apply for your practice so long as you expect to stay in one location for a considerable period.

The location of such a building and its appropriateness for your practice should be the overriding criteria for such a decision, but the investment potential and its value should also be considered. This is important, especially if you plan for your practice to expand in size and therefore in the required office or clinic area. If the building you purchase becomes too small to house your practice, its location needs to lend itself to being readily rented out to someone else. In other words, you need to see this option as a long-term investment and a wealth-creation strategy at the same time as a practice development strategy. If you were to select this option you need to be comfortable with becoming a landlord and all that this responsibility entails.

The main advantages of owning the building from which you practise is that you, as the landlord, receive income from the practice income. The two practical ways of achieving this objective, with little extra cash, are: first, through a loan secured against equity in your home (or some other investment you own); and, second, through the use of your pension fund (refer to discussion on wealth creation in Chapter 3). The pension option assumes that you operate your own fund that, when properly structured, can purchase and rent a building to your practice at commercial rates.

One point that you need to check for the second option is whether or not your pension fund can borrow money. Your accountant would need to advise you on the available options, which might include the set-up of a special trust that can issue monetary units to the fund. Furthermore, investment decisions must be conducted at arm's length from your practice needs, always aiming to achieve the maximum benefit for pension fund members (that is, yourself and other members of the scheme) rather than your business. This second option is clearly quite complex and you would be well advised to seek opinion and assistance from suitably qualified professionals. It is presented here as a demonstration of one of many innovative ways to locate premises of high quality that can be either done very economically or with long-term investment in mind.

4.4.7 Forensic calls

Sometimes you will be consulted away from your practice. In particular, as a practising psychologist you are always liable to be called to court. Although the probability of a non-forensic psychologist being called is not high, it is always a possibility. To psychologists unaccustomed to vigorously defending an approach or a position, or to withstanding a full and frank inquiry, this can be a chastening experience. Given that the presenting of records or personal attendance at court can be compelled, the urge to keep everything orderly and professionally done is most important.

One of the authors recalls a cross-examination in court in which the reliability of an IQ score was questioned: 'Tell me, Mr X, you obtained a score of 110 on that occasion? If it were done on another occasion, would the score be the same?' Mr X answered that it would be substantially the same. 'How much the same?' pursued the barrister. This led to an account of the probability of sampling errors, of attitudinal factors, and of motivation. The barrister then discomfited the psychologist by asking that he explain the statistical concepts underlying time samples of an IQ: 'In simple terms that the jury would understand. While you are doing that, perhaps you would be kind enough to clarify for the court the concepts of sampling errors, the standard error of the mean, and the various forms of reliability that psychologists use.' This approach was clearly meant to be at once a clarification for the court and a means of testing the knowledge and the professional steel of the psychologist. At its worst it was meant to show discredit to a psychologist who could not answer satisfactorily.

If summoned to court, the one thing to bear in mind is to be the independent professional. The psychologist is not there as a client's representative but rather as a professional whose knowledge can assist the court to reach a just conclusion. Answering truthfully is paramount; answering with knowledge and confidence is a huge bonus.

4.5 Insurances

One fundamental task that you need to undertake prior to the commencement of your practice is to take out insurances to provide the necessary cover in case of any adverse and unforeseen circumstances. As a minimum, you should have current insurance policies at any time during the operation of your practice for professional indemnity, public liability, and fire and theft for your practice premises. Additionally, if you employ anyone, they should be appropriately covered through employers' liability insurance. It is important to note that if you operate your practice from home, your home insurance may not cover items used for income generation, as they would normally attract a commercial rate.

It is recommended that you seek advice from an independent insurance broker regarding vital insurance policies. A broker can usually obtain the least-expensive rate for your insurance needs. Having said that, professional indemnity insurance is very competitively provided by the insurance firm providing a policy package for British Psychological Society members. Other major insurance companies also provide professional indemnity insurance for psychologists (see Appendix B).

In the area of personal insurance needs, you should also consider the levels of your current policy cover for life insurance, income protection, and disability cover. When your income is totally dependent on your capacity to work, and when you are no longer protected by an employer's provisions, it is up to you to insure your income ability. You will need to weigh up your personal situation, taking into account the level of debt that you are exposed to, your personal and family needs, the period of time you can survive with no income, and the cost of each insurance. In this area your financial adviser may be the best source of assistance. You may also consider joining a health fund: a severe illness could erode your capital and put the business at risk.

A list of insurances that you should consider is given in various places. A document put out by NatWest Bank provides a valuable list (NatWest, 1999). A modified version of that source is as follows for insurance types you should consider:

- buildings (check if rented premises already covered, and for what);
- contents;
- money: cash on premises and in transit, fidelity coverage for those dealing with cash;
- vehicles;
- public liability;
- product liability (e.g., own-developed psychometric tests, biofeedback equipment, etc.);
- employer's liability;
- professional indemnity and malpractice cover, and legal expenses;
- income: loss of chartered psychologist status, inability to work;
- personal: loan protection, director's indemnity, private health insurance, and business travel.

It must be appreciated that insurance exists in a commercially competitive world. Insurance companies and brokers vie for business. It is the reputation of the insuring organization, the cost of premiums, the coverage that such policies offer, and the probity of the way in which the insurance companies deal with claims that all determine the value of a policy. If there is a claim over a certain sum, a 'loss adjuster' could be involved. Honesty is always a good policy. Recall, too, that the insurance company ultimately pays loss adjusters.

4.6 Communication systems

Irrespective of what sort of premises you choose for your practice, you will need to address its communication systems. These comprise the means by which your clients will be able to contact you, and how and when you will return their calls if you are unavailable. In particular, if your practice depends on seeing clients face to face, the question that you need to answer clearly is: 'What process will my potential clients go through to make appointments with me?'

While it is acceptable in a corporate world to place a call to a professional who is not always available, leave a message and have the call returned, this is not the case with members of the general public who wish to make appointments with a professional psychologist. Their expectation is that the process of booking an appointment will be relatively painless. For a client from amongst the general public, and for a corporate client – and that includes referrers of clients – you need to establish foolproof systems of communication.

The authors are intimately aware of a significant gap in this fundamental area of business conduct of many psychologists (from their personal attempts to systematically contact groups of practising colleagues, using the phone numbers provided by practitioners as their business contact numbers). If psychology as a profession is to improve its standing in the community, this area needs to be dramatically improved in the next decade. No business can operate in isolation from the outside world, particularly one that provides services to the public. Some large corporations have estimated, as part of their risk-management exercise, that they would be out of business within days if their telephone systems suddenly stopped functioning. This is just as true of professional service business.

There is more to effective communication systems built into a successful business than listing a telephone number on which the practitioner is sometimes available. The aim is to achieve the highest quality of each transaction between your practice and the client – or anyone who chooses to contact your practice for that matter. In designing communication solutions for your business, you may wish to consider the following checklist of questions that will most likely be processed by your clients, even if quite unconsciously:

- How long does it take for the phone to be answered?
- How is the phone answered – does it seem professional?
- Does the receptionist clearly identify the practice?
- Is the receptionist's manner warm and courteous?
- Is the client's query handled to their satisfaction?
- Is the client given immediate options if the person they phoned (most likely yourself) is unavailable?
- How long does it take for the client's call to be returned?
- How many times is the phone engaged when the client telephones?

In this era of a communications revolution, there are many cost-effective and readily available options that are particularly geared to small businesses. The choices explored below assume that you do not employ someone whose sole responsibility is to answer the telephone and that you are a sole practitioner in the initial practice set-up phase. It is further assumed that you cannot answer all the calls yourself since you are either engaged on professional matters or out of the office.

4.6.1 Easy call systems

One of the simplest ways in which to overcome the problem of an engaged telephone is to contract a phone-answering service to answer on your behalf. To find out more, simply contact the company providing your telephone services. As long as the exchange in your area has such capabilities, and you have a touchtone phone, it is usually only a matter of requesting the extra service (and paying for it). It does not involve any extra cable connections. The way in which this dual line operates is that, when another caller dials your line while you are engaged in another telephone conversation, you can hear a distinct tone. You can either ask the first caller to wait, or terminate the call. Then, by pressing appropriate designated buttons on your touchtone phone, you can connect with the second caller.

One of the disadvantages of this system is that you only have a limited number of rings before the second call becomes unavailable to you, and as far as that caller is concerned you did not answer the call. This is probably the worst scenario in the business customer-relations sense. When your phone is engaged, potential clients might give you another chance and try again if they really want to reach you, but when it seems that you do not answer your phone at all, the message is as good as: 'I am out of business'. Further, while this option may solve the problem of the engaged phone, it does nothing to help you communicate with your clients while you are busy with other business activities. You will need other technology to assist with this common problem of a small professional practice.

4.6.2 Telephone answering machines

The simplest yet least effective way to deal with the problem of the sole practitioner's unavailability is a telephone answering machine. Despite the penetration of answering machines into the marketplace, there are many people who react with some anxiety when they need to record their message on tape. It seems logical that this problem will be more frequently experienced by the specific target group of a psychologist's clients in a clinical or a counselling setting.

Intuitively, it would seem that a client who phones to make an appointment for a problem of a psychological nature is not likely to leave a coherent message on an answering machine. They will also, understandably, not want to leave a spoken record for non-professionals (receptionists and others) to overhear, and they might not be prepared to leave their name and phone number without an assurance of confidentiality.

If you choose, therefore, to include an answering machine within your business communication system, it is useful to select one that enables you to listen to messages remotely. You do this by simply dialling your own number and then dialling a personal identification number when your greeting is heard. Most telephones now utilize pulse-dial exchange technology, which means that you need only to press telephone buttons to send the secret code to your answering machine. If the telephone you are using to remotely obtain your messages does not have such capability, you can purchase a small numerical pad that will enable message retrieval from any phone. This is especially useful when travelling in remote locations, and when using public phones to check your messages.

Most answering machines also have a way of informing you whether or not any messages have been recorded, which means that you need actually pay for a long-distance call to pick up your messages only when you can be sure that a message has been recorded. When you record your greeting on the answering machine you need to consider the listener's perceptions. It needs to encourage them to leave a message rather than hang up, so it needs to be friendly, but professional at the same time. It cannot be too long, so that a long-distance or mobile phone caller does not get frustrated at the wasted cost of a call.

The usually accepted form of a greeting message includes these components:

- introduction of the practice name;
- a short apology for not being personally available;
- encouragement and reminder to leave the caller's name and phone number;

- a short statement of commitment that the call will be returned;
- a quick reassurance that the caller is important to you.

It may also pay to monitor how your greeting message is received by callers. It is often possible to note how many callers hung up without leaving a message. One way of checking the effectiveness of your system is simply to ask a sample of your callers how comfortable they felt about leaving their messages. If your answering machine (or phone, for that matter) is used by others (for example, your family), your greeting message, irrespective of whether it is delivered by a person or a machine, should take your business into consideration.

Your income is inextricably linked with your ability to maximize each call of a potential customer. It is therefore proposed that you consider your communication systems seriously in your strategy for growth when developing a business plan. There are other systems currently available that do not attract high costs. These are explored below in detail.

4.6.3 Voice mail

Voice mail is really another version of an answering machine except that, rather than using cassette tape-recording facilities, the messages are recorded through digital technology. These are usually available on business telephone systems. Other voice mail services are also provided by various mobile phone companies, which divert the callers to your voice mailbox if the mobile phone is either engaged, switched off or out of reach.

The more sophisticated telephone systems also have the capacity for the messages to be stored in a voice mailbox for different people in an office, who then retrieve their messages via their office phones. Voice mail facilities enable you to record your personal greeting via your telephone and then maintain your messages by either saving or deleting them; also, the same can be achieved by specially designated codes sent by your phone. As far as the caller is concerned, the effect is the same as the popularly known and accepted answering machine technology.

4.6.4 Electronic pagers

Electronic pagers have been around for more than a decade. It is to be noted that many new mobile phones fulfil the functions once filled by pagers. Pagers have become smaller and so should be secured to something like a belt or else they tend to get lost. They began to be used mainly in medical and emergency environments, by sending just a beep to the holder who was then obliged to phone a central agency or a designated phone number to receive the message. Their sophistication grew in the late 1980s to include alphanumeric characters as part of the message being transmitted to, and received directly by, the pager.

This is an excellent example of a one-way communication, not unlike writing a letter but far more immediate. At the lowest level of the current technology, the caller dials a given phone number, quotes your pager number (usually six digits), and then communicates his message, which the operator immediately transmits to you. Your pager beeps continuously, beeps intermittently, flashes and/or vibrates, depending on the type and setting you have selected. It is probably best to train yourself to receive and react with discretion to either beeping or vibrating messages to maximize the value of this technology.

The great advantage of receiving one-way pager messages is that you can respond to the caller at the most convenient time. The downside is the impersonal nature of the caller interacting with an operator, and the requirement to quote your pager number.

4.6.5 *Personalized pager answering services*

There are variations of electronic pager technology that have greatly enhanced the initial dialling of your number and the interaction between the caller and the operator. Rather than having to remember and quote your pager number, it is possible for the caller to simply dial what looks like a normal phone number (but in fact some of its digits are your personal identifiers), and hear the call answered in the name of your practice or your personal name, according to your instructions to the pager service company. Thus, the client's impression is that your assistant or a receptionist has answered the call.

At this point of client and telephone operator interaction, the service quality provided by paging companies can make an enormous difference to your business. Some companies take their client (that is yourself as the client now) satisfaction very seriously, and they respond to your needs as a small business operator. They train their staff to answer calls professionally, they monitor the number of times a phone has to ring before it is answered, and they respond by providing more operators at peak times. Even more importantly, they hold any other information about you and your practice to pass on to your callers as per your instructions. For example, this could include your practice address, what your business does, or your fax number.

Furthermore, if a client phones and asks a general question without specifically asking to page you, the operator's response will be something like this: 'I'm sorry, I cannot help you but I can get someone to call you back', and they promptly take the caller's name, phone number and pass on this information to you via your pager. It is easy to keep a check on them by simply phoning your own pager service and monitoring their operators' responses. There are some (unfortunately) who will simply answer: 'We are only a pager service'. Choose the operator company carefully.

While the pager-frequency transmission technologies are very reliable, they are not totally foolproof. Some messages can be missed or get directed to the wrong pager. If, for some reason, your pager was switched off, its battery was low or you were in an unreachable spot, it is possible to phone the 'message recall' operator service that will read out the last few messages for you. Beware of putting your pager near a computer or electrical system: your messages may get scrambled. At an extra cost, a printed copy of the last messages, usually limited to a given number of days, can also be obtained.

A useful habit to develop is always to check the sequential number of your messages so that if one message is missed you can become immediately aware of this and follow it up with the operator. Another helpful routine, which will minimize the potential problems, is to replace the battery on a regular basis – for example, on the first day of each month – rather than waiting for the 'battery low' signal.

Pager coverage is another factor that you will need to carefully manage and monitor. If you are travelling in country areas, other than the ones designated for your pager service, it is likely that you will miss some messages. It is possible to request that, for those limited times, the pager coverage gets extended to 'follow you'. Alternatively, if you travel on a frequent basis in areas where reception is difficult, you may choose instead a larger coverage, such as 'national', at the extra cost, and this will be more efficient than having to request the extension each time you travel.

The total costs of such a service include the initial investment of the pager, depending on its type, size and functions. Companies providing paging services usually provide pagers. The basic service, where the callers have to quote your pager number, is cheaper than the additional service of personalized answering by the operator. The prices will vary if you have a number of pagers connected to the personalized answering service and if you request a coverage that is greater than the one standard area. The total annual cost of having your telephone answered professionally and courteously at all times, 24 hours per day, can be inexpensive when compared to the cost of engaging a secretary/receptionist.

Digital mobile phones can also act as pagers. This is, comparatively, a very cost-efficient system, when you consider the costs of purchasing your own telephone system, its normal ongoing costs, and the full-time salary. You may be ready to embrace the idea but do not wish to have this sort of service as your only option – you might, for example, wish to answer your own telephone when you are available, and use the answering service when you are otherwise engaged, but you do not wish to advertise many different phone numbers to your clients. Simple solutions to this real dilemma are provided in the discussion of telephone diversions below.

The drawback for those professionals whose clients need to make an appointment or change a previously made appointment is that even a personalized pager answering service cannot replace someone who has access to your diary. If your business is predominantly geared to providing one-to-one counselling services, a shared receptionist with a dedicated task of arranging appointments for you would seem a far more effective option than returning all the calls sent to you via the pager. You will also need to consider that you may have to attempt to return some callers' messages a number of times before reaching them.

4.6.6 Mobile phones

Mobile phones have become widely accepted as a norm in our society in a relatively few years. They can now fit in your pocket, and the smallest phone in the world at the time of writing is as small as a pager. Since their smallness has now reached the ergonomic limits of having to hold them in your hand, their size will probably not decrease any further. What will most probably occur, however, is the mobile takeover from other normal phones. Once the communications networks become more extensive and reliable, there is likely to be one phone for every person rather than one for every home.

The mobile phone has revolutionized the way business is conducted to an even greater extent than the fax did in the past. It has increased customers' expectations of the immediacy of everyone's availability, particularly in the service industry. This has added extra pressures as far as business competitiveness is concerned, and set new standards. Professionals providing psychology (or any other personalized services), particularly in the corporate sector, have to be aware of these expectations.

As long as your communication systems overall are such that you are able to respond to your clients' calls and satisfactorily deal with their needs, you may never need a mobile. There is also an argument that if a professional is too readily available they send an implicit message to their callers that they do not have much work. There is a need for a subtle balance between satisfying clients' expectations and not becoming a slave to the mobile phone.

It is not a purpose of this book to explore the etiquette of using mobile phones, but the user must be aware of the effect that conducting a conversation on the mobile phone has on those nearby. If, for example, you are in a meeting with a client or at lunch with another person, answering your mobile phone tends to send an undesirable message to them that they are not as important as your caller. You need to resist answering your phone every time it rings, but one may argue that this seems to defeat the purpose of having a mobile phone. This depends on the purpose for which you choose to use the mobile technology. More specifically, it is your decision whether you control it and use it as a tool to achieve your business strategies or whether it controls your behaviour.

One purpose that a mobile phone fulfils impeccably is to utilize your spare time to return your clients' calls when you would normally not be able to do so. It can also add to the flexibility of your lifestyle without compromising your business. If a mobile phone adds value to your lifestyle by enabling you to play golf, or sail more often, then it serves a useful purpose. If it interrupts the few moments that you have set aside for relaxation and recovery, then it is time to switch it off.

4.6.7 Telephone diversions

The overall communications system that you will develop to suit your business purposes can utilize the combination of all of the preceding technologies. In the current competitive economic climate and with the rapid development of even newer technologies, these systems will only function to their full effectiveness when you link them with appropriate diversion facilities.

Telephone diversion technologies enable you to have the best of all options. On the one hand, you can answer calls personally when you are available; on the other hand, when you are not available, the phone may be answered by someone else such as your personalized pager service operator or, at worst, your voice mail or some other machine.

Furthermore, it is possible to have a number of diversion layers. For example, as the first choice, when you are away from your normal practice phone, the initial diversion could connect the caller to your mobile phone. When your mobile phone is engaged, the caller could then be diverted to your pager answering operator. In this way, you can maximize your availability to your clients, especially at the early stage of your business development when you have some spare time to answer your calls. At the same time you eliminate any potential for your clients to find your phone engaged or unanswered.

There are four types of phone diversions, all of which fulfil different purposes at various times:

- total diversion of all calls;
- on engaged;

- on unanswered;
- on 'out of range' or switched off (for mobile phones).

The diversion facilities are obtained by requesting them from the main provider of your telephone system. They are activated at the telephone exchange, assuming they have such capacity, and so there is no need for substantial investment in special equipment, as was the case only a few years ago. The charges for such diversion facilities are made on a call-by-call basis and they are so minimal that most often they are totally overshadowed by all other telephone costs.

Permanent diversions are also of great benefit when you move your practice to new premises. For the initial period of time it is useful to activate a total diversion from the old to the new practice number, in order to allow you some time to inform all your clients and change the numbers in all the advertisements and on your stationery. By monitoring the number of diversions actually activated each month on the phone bill, you can phase out this relatively inexpensive facility when it is no longer being used by a significant number of calls.

Another service available for such purposes is a permanent recorded message that identifies your practice and provides the caller with a new number to ring. And an even less expensive and lower-level service is a general recorded message, which instructs the caller to contact the telephone system service provider to obtain the new number.

4.6.8 Fax machines

In connection with planning your business communication systems, it is the facsimile (fax) machine that has become the standard in the corporate world over the last decade. It fulfils quite a different function from a telephone system and is an additional rather than an alternative consideration.

While it may still be regarded as an optional facility, it is more the norm than the exception. It is not uncommon for virtually anyone – including some individual clients who need to communicate some report to you – to expect that a fax machine is available. Thus the question may be asked: 'What is your fax number?' rather than 'Do you have a fax machine?' This is especially so since phone/fax machines have become accepted into people's homes.

There are a number of inexpensive alternatives that should be considered as part of your overall communication system. If you have an aversion to 'new' technology and prefer not to invest in a fax machine, you may choose to set up an arrangement with someone in your local proximity who offers a public fax service. The cost of each fax received will be greater, you will probably be charged per page of fax received, and the extra service may involve being phoned when a fax has been received on your behalf. This way, you can make the fax facility available to your clients without actually owning a machine – but be wary of professional confidentiality under this arrangement. This option, of course, is only feasible if you do not expect many faxes coming in or going out.

When you have made too many trips to your public fax, or are frustrated by their unavailability outside the hours they choose to be open, you will be ready to embrace this technology as one of the inevitabilities of doing business in the twenty-first century. Then, the next-level option is to a combined phone/fax machine. Such a gadget uses one telephone plug and 'intelligently' works out whether the incoming call is a fax or a person and answers accordingly, and that means you do not need to have a separate telephone line dedicated to the fax machine.

If you have already purchased separate 'boxes' as most people have – a telephone and a fax machine that have not been joined together in the factory – you will need a 'fax switch' to enable the fax machine to switch on if a fax comes in when you are not there to answer it. We advise against this option. The switch boxes and sharing of phone and fax lines was quite acceptable in the early 1980s when the technology of the time required the person to initiate the call and then press the fax button. Since the current technology expects machines – including computers (see below) – to be talking to each other, a much more efficient method is to connect your fax machine to a dedicated telephone line and relax. This will add to the cost of your practice set-up, however, and so it must be weighed against the potential.

If you are about to choose a fax machine, the main difference between them is the use of plain paper with laser technology and thermal paper. While the thermal paper machine is likely to be cheaper, you will need to consider the cost of photocopying each received fax if you need the contents to last for more than a few months. For, when thermally sensitive paper is exposed to sunlight, it tends to fade relatively quickly. Filing these pages will prolong the thermal fax life a little, but you can still expect to look at almost blank pages after a few years.

Another alternative to purchasing a dedicated fax machine is a computer fax, which is linked to a modem, as discussed below. The main advantage of a computer fax modem comes when the document to be faxed is computer-generated. For example, if you have word-processed a letter or report and then you need to fax it, you can fax it directly from your computer rather than having to print it and then fax it. In most cases you will probably choose to print it anyway for your file records, but you will still save time on the faxing process if a significant number of pages need to be faxed.

The main limitation of a computer fax is that if you would like to fax anything not generated by a computer, it first needs to be scanned to enable its fax transmission – and for that you need a scanner. Also, unless your computer is switched on, you will not be able to receive incoming faxes: there is no 'fax mailbox' facility, so far, in the ether.

4.6.9 Electronic mail

Electronic mail, popularly referred to as email, has also become embraced by our society as a norm. This technology requires the availability of a computer with a modem; in addition, you will need an internet service provider (ISP).

There are an increasing number of service providers who essentially make available to you a space on their computer. The public connection to their computer, which is expected to operate 24 hours a day every day, enables it to receive messages and documents emailed to you, and the other way around. Others communicate with you by accessing a dedicated email address which uniquely identifies yourself. The information that belongs to you is stored on the ISP's master computer for a limited period of time, and you can access it as often as you wish, to check whether any messages have arrived for you, and whenever you want to send a message to someone else.

The real power in utilizing this technology is its speed and its ability to deliver whole documents in a computer format, by 'attaching' them to your email messages, which others can immediately continue to edit or print. While this is not likely to excite your individual clients, it is potentially a real advantage when dealing with corporate clients. They can be provided with training materials, assessment reports or other documents you might be asked to prepare, all via their internal email system networks ('intranets'), which can usually communicate with public email boxes as well.

Another application of such communication is collaborative project work that you might be undertaking with a consortium of colleagues. Your time can be most efficiently used when you can communicate via email, which enables you to edit parts of various documents without necessarily printing them. This communication should not be confused with the Internet itself, which is really a network of computers around the world. Whereas computers providing email facilities and access to the Internet may be the same, in most cases email is quite a different channel of two-way communication.

4.7 Initial marketing

Having planned, selected and established a communication system that suits your business and satisfies your clients' needs, you will be ready to promote your business. You will now have some assurance that if the promotion works and calls start coming in, your business will have the capacity to respond to those calls and to actually provide the services.

There are a number of ways in which marketing of the practice can be put into practical effect. Some of these methods are described further in the remainder of this section. Your attention is also drawn, in connection with marketing, to companies designed to make small and medium-sized businesses more competitive by helping them make better use of information and communications technology (e.g., Technology Means Business [Appendix B] and others available via the web).

4.7.1 Promotional brochures

One of the first steps of most practitioners when they set up in business is to produce a brochure whose contents present an outline of the services that the practice provides. Although it might be possible to develop a successful practice without such a promotional tool, producing one will certainly help you crystallize in your own mind what your business really sells. It will also be helpful when others to whom you will be promoting your business ask you about what your practice actually does.

Before you ask a graphic designer or a desktop publisher to assist you with the generation of your first marketing material, you need to be quite certain of what you would like to present in it. In addition to the obvious identification of your practice, with your name, logo, address and contact details, it may include:

- how your services will assist your client;
- what services you provide;
- what other organizations have received your services, if it is directed to organizations;
- who you are and what credibility you have to provide such services;
- how you go about providing your services; and possibly
- how much you charge for your services, and permitted methods of payment.

There are many different formats of promotional brochures, the most common of which is an A4 sheet printed across the long edge (in a landscape format) and folded in three (making six panels by using both sides). There are many variations of this basic format, including two A4 sheets (i.e., an A3 sheet folded in half) or an A4 sheet slightly reduced in size. Some graphic designers, printers, desktop publishers and marketing experts will propose more creative designs to ensure that your brochure stands out and is noticed. This is a reasonable proposition which you may wish to explore when planning your brochure and content design.

First, however, you need to identify the purpose for which the brochure will be used. For example, are you planning to mail it directly to a number of businesses, individuals, schools or clinics? If so, will you include a letter with it or does the brochure stand on its own? Alternatively, you may always hand-deliver the brochure, which will allow you to introduce and draw the attention of the reader to the parts that are more relevant to them. If you are planning to post out the brochure, you will need to invest some effort and creativity in its design to ensure that it receives the attention it deserves.

As with your letterheads, the design and content of your brochure will reflect your business and life values. These messages will be decoded by the reader in terms of your commitment to quality, your innovative capacity, and the value of your services. Most readers of marketing material, it seems, are preoccupied with one big question that can be expressed as: 'What's in it for me?' Your promotional material must somehow answer this question or else it will miss its mark.

This realization that your marketing must be focused on client need can revolutionize your thinking and your design. With this new paradigm, you can no longer design brochures talking about yourself but rather about how your services are designed to provide real value to the reader.

If your practice provides a number of different services, some of which may be more suitable to some clients than others, and you would prefer to build some flexibility in to your promotional brochure, you may consider printing one overall summary brochure with each service outlined on separate pages. This approach will enable you to selectively distribute your marketing material in a targeted way to the identified groups of your clients, and in this way you should be able to maximize its impact. Further, if you have a number of sheets each outlining a different service, you may wish to design the summary brochure in such a way that it contains a pocket for the individual sheets.

Be mindful of the ethics of advertising. In particular, see the section of the British Psychological Society's Code of Professional Conduct (2000) dealing with advertising. Page 22 of the BPS *Code of Conduct, Ethical Principles and Guidelines* gives clear instruction under the heading 'Guidelines on Advertising the Services Offered by Psychologists'.

Advertised services must be within your competence and must not guarantee results, particularly if directed to the general public: it is to be remembered that professions usually charge on the basis of fee-for-service – not fee-for-outcome.

Psychological practitioners might think of a number of creative ways of bringing their services to public notice. Provided that they conform to the BPS Guidelines mentioned in the previous paragraph, every encouragement is given to think of extra ways of so doing. Readers who are attracted to novel ways of promoting might consider consulting a book by Haywood (1998) on 'do-it-yourself' public relations.

4.7.2 Targeted distribution

One of the most fundamental business principles is to inform the marketplace about the products that you have for sale. If your brochure serves as a product catalogue, you will need to ensure that it gets into the hands of potential clients or referrers of clients. The distribution of your brochures will produce better results per pound spent if you carefully target your readership.

In such targeting, you select that sector of the market that, in your view, or according to your market research, will have the greatest need for your services. For example, you may distribute to medical practitioners in your local geographical area rather than all over metropolitan or country areas, because you believe that that grouping is more likely to be interested in referring their patients locally. If you are targeting an organization, you may select a group by industry sector, number of employees, type of organization – government, private or community association – or by geographical area.

Depending on your marketing plan, you may start with a small distribution (100 brochures, say) and then conduct an intensive follow-up of all the brochures. Alternatively, you may decide to begin with a distribution of a large number of brochures and selectively follow up those you feel will produce best results. In all of your direct mail distributions, it is quite realistic to estimate your results on the basis of 1 per cent of all the recipients of letters and/or brochures being interested in what you offer, with 0.5 per cent being ready to purchase your product. You can obtain far better results by careful targeting of your material to those potential clients who have the greatest need or who can readily identify with your practice or your product.

You may well achieve better percentages, but it does not pay to expect them. By being more conservative in your estimates, you will avoid disappointments and will be able to plan the distribution of your promotional material more effectively. The most common mistake that practitioners tend to make is to underestimate the amount of material they need to distribute in order to achieve a reasonable client basis from which to commence a workable practice.

If you are planning a direct mail distribution you need to keep in mind that your material is unsolicited. To increase its chances of being opened and read, it needs to somehow stand out from the rest of the advertising material finding its way to each desk every day. You yourself probably receive unsolicited advertising material at your home. This is because some business marketing experts have identified you as a person in their target market. When you open the next advertising brochure that appears on your desk, you may ask yourself this question: 'What made me open this one and look at it?' If you have gone further and purchased the advertised product, the next useful question is: 'What was in that brochure that made me want to buy the product or service?'

Royal Mail has customer lists but they are not available to the public. Lists are, however, available from so-called 'list brokers'. In *Yellow Pages* they may be found under Direct Mail. The Direct Marketing Association keeps a list of reputable brokers.

4.7.3 Personal follow-up

There is clear evidence that if you include a personalized letter with your promotional literature and if you follow up its distribution in person, you greatly increase its chances of success.

One of the facts of a people-based business providing intangible products is that the buyer of such a product is unlikely to choose the provider randomly. There are many factors that guide the potential clients' selection processes, but one of the foremost must be confidence in the provider and trust in their capability to provide the service they promised. In this light, it is far better to think of all your marketing exercises as relationship building with referrers of your clients, or 'gatekeepers'. Such relationship-based marketing takes time to produce results, and so you will need some patience; but it is a far surer way to succeed. Such relationships can begin by simply following up the initial letters or brochures you send out. To conduct such a follow-up, you begin by simply making a telephone call to the recipient of your marketing letter and requesting a meeting so that you can explain your services more personally. Some persistence will be necessary at times to make the first few appointments. When you have built up some experience of such meetings, you will go into new ones with some confidence.

It is most important to be prepared for such telephone contacts and introductory meetings. By preparing and practising each conversation, you will feel far more in charge of the situation. When you attend an introductory meeting with your potential referrer or corporate client, you are likely to leave a more positive impression if you take time to listen to your interviewee's perspective, and particularly their needs, rather than just presenting your services.

Once you have commenced a contact with your potential referrers, it is important to maintain it so that your presence in the marketplace remains. They may not have had anyone or any project to refer to you at the time when you called. Your aim is to have them continue to be aware of your services, so that when they *do* have a need, they can form an immediate association between their need and your practice.

4.7.4 Phone book advertising

Advertising in British Telecom's *Yellow Pages* (or equivalent) is one of those expenses that may be worthwhile. If you have a business number, the basic entry is free and you may pay to have your advert extended, line-blocked, or enhanced with graphics. There are different sections in *Yellow Pages* under which you can place your advertisement.

Under 'Psychologists' there is a section that simply lists the name of your practice within the alphabetical order of advertisers. If you are a Chartered Psychologist, then you might apply to appear in the subsection of Psychologists that uses the British Psychological Society's logo and is headed 'Chartered Psychologists'. Other entries might be under 'Psychometric Testing and Assessment', or 'Psychotherapy and Analysis'. For those in business consulting, the headings of 'Management & Business Consultants', or 'Business Consultants' might be appropriate. These you need to pay for separately, and you need to contact the relevant association (e.g., the BPS) to be included in the listing.

The British Psychological Society listing provides an assurance to the public using *Yellow Pages* as a guide that the listed psychologists are British Psychological Society members. While there is no known research about the effectiveness of these advertisements, there is anecdotal evidence that being listed under your association tends to produce better results. Practitioners tend to agree that advertising in telephone directories does not always produce immediate – or even long-term – visible results. Nevertheless, most practitioners choose to advertise in this way, more for the purpose of establishing credibility: whereas practitioners accept that clients are unlikely to select them on some random basis from *Yellow Pages*(or equivalent), it is where clients often check whether someone has the credentials they claim to have.

If, on the other hand, your practice or name is already known to potential clients, they are more likely to choose you rather than use a random selection. Building your public image is therefore important for long-term success. If potential clients search for a psychologist and have no other means of choosing one, they tend to select on the basis of their geographical proximity. Hence, your local guide is also more likely to produce results. Being seen in the *Yellow Pages* or other business telephone directories is one of the first steps in setting up your practice – although by itself this investment might or might not generate any significant income.

4.7.5 Newspaper advertising

In general, building relationships with a potential referrer of individual clients or projects is by far the most effective marketing exercise. There is a place for advertising in your marketing plan for the purpose of building a name that is recognized by potential clients. For example, if you make an appointment to see someone as a follow-up of your brochure, they are more likely to agree to see you if they have recognized the name or logo from somewhere else. The recognition factor tends to work even if they cannot exactly recall where they had become aware of your practice. This phenomenon occurs more powerfully through the television medium, although that particular medium may not be the most appropriate method of communicating for professional psychology practices.

It nevertheless makes sense, particularly in the early stages, to place some advertisements – although it is recommended that this be done carefully rather than extravagantly. And even though signing up long-term ongoing ads may be cheaper per placement, it may be difficult to get out of the arrangement when you discover that the desired result has not come about. Most practitioners tend to use local newspapers in order to build an image in the geographical area in which they practise.

4.7.6 Using local media

In addition to advertising in the local newspaper, you may wish to explore other means of utilizing the local media to communicate your message without having to pay for it. The way this works is that local newspapers, like any other media, search for newsworthy items in order to fill their editorial pages. If you are involved in some practice activity, such as a seminar, a group or a free talk about a specific subject, this may be newsworthy.

To communicate this to the local paper you will need to contact a local journalist and discuss it with her or him. If you provide a simple summary of what the activity is, you will find that by helping the journalist you may increase the chances of publication.

Another way in which you can generate a public image through the local media is by writing articles or letters on a particular subject that may be of general interest. The current interest in issues relating to psychology is increasing rapidly, and most newspapers will cooperate with you as long as you have something of interest to say, and you are not seen to be just promoting your services. See Haywood (1998) for such an approach.

It is important to distinguish between promoting your services and increasing your public recognition in the marketplace. Both activities are important, but the latter is an ongoing activity that generates an advantageous environment for the marketing of your services. If you would like to benefit more from dealing with the media, you may find it useful to increase your skills in handling media interviews through various seminars which are generally available through professional development programmes or as workshops associated with psychology conferences.

4.7.7 Using the Internet

Nowadays, in the twenty-first century, it is very easy also to advertise a business using the Internet. Internet service providers generally provide their customers with computer space for holding a website, on which a business can advertise itself to the wider world. As stated above, most psychology practices wish to advertise themselves only for a very local clientele, but a literally worldwide presence for very little cost – website designers can be contracted to construct something for you, or you can do something yourself through ISP-supplied software – is well worth considering. (See also section 4.11.3.)

4.8 Fee schedules

Appendix D has been constructed to give an indication of the relative value of your time for different aspects of your professional services. Taking the one-hour consultation as standard, the relative costs of other variants of consulting are proposed, which take time, effort, and extra costs into account. It is not held that this is an immutable list, rather it is a working schedule that practitioners might wish to use and to adapt to their own special circumstances.

4.8.1 Recognizing your own value

Psychologists have traditionally struggled with placing the appropriate price-tag on their product. A number of psychologists in private practice have other jobs, some of them full time. Some have been providing services from their homes. Partly because of such a historical basis, the fees actually charged in the marketplace have varied widely. The part-time practitioners who had other income and who had no administrative overheads associated with running a full-time practice have been able to discount charge rates.

Another factor resulting in psychologists' ambivalence in charging high fees has been the recognition that some clients cannot afford professional psychology fees and therefore would have no access to such services unless fees are discounted. And some quasi-psychology services have been provided elsewhere (some religious denominations, and some local councils, for example). In such a climate it has been easy to underestimate the value of psychological services, particularly given their intangible nature.

On the other hand, the marketing professionals have been sending another message to psychologists. In essence, their message has been: 'People will pay high prices for anything that satisfies their needs, as long as they can perceive its value.' What is the value of better relationships, better health, better performance at work, better functioning teams, the ability to get a job, and the ability to think more effectively and therefore lead more effective lives? If you ask your clients to put a price tag on your products, you may be surprised to learn their perception is different from yours.

In order to get some idea of how careers in psychology pay in reality, readers are recommended to the British Psychological Society's 1999 pamphlet entitled *Careers in Psychology.* You, as a service provider, need to be comfortable with charging reasonable fees, in order to reward you for the effort you have exerted in providing that service as well as for the time you have spent accumulating knowledge, skills and experience. All of these factors combine to enable you to provide the sorts of services that your clients need and from which they benefit. In setting your fees, you must believe in the worth of your services.

Once you have internalized the recognition of such value in your own product, the next step, of telling the client how much they have to pay, should be relatively easy. Marketing experts suggest that you may even help your clients by explicitly pointing out the value of the services they have just received. This can be done perhaps even more appropriately by a well-trained receptionist.

4.8.2 Setting your fees

It will be appreciated by readers that fees change with time, with legislation, and with market demand. In order to help the practitioner set proportional fees, Appendix D gives a set of suggestions, which take the basic fee for an hour's consultation and then give the suggested percentages of variations (as mentioned above).

The calculation of an underlying hourly rate will be based on a number of assumptions. These include the psychologist operating a full-time practice and incurring all the staff-, administration- and premises-related costs. When all the expenses and reasonable chargeable time are entered into the equation, this rate generates income that is commensurate with a senior clinician's salary. If, however, a particular psychologist does not operate such a practice, it could be considered that the savings in overhead costs might be passed on to consumers rather than retained as profit for the practitioner.

It should be noted that the rates set will be for face-to-face contact. There is an assumption that the productivity rate is about two-thirds of contact time. The remaining one-third is taken up with making notes, administration connected with the consultation, and other overheads.

It is quite acceptable and good practice to reflect different types of service and client status in a sliding scale of fees. For example, you may apply different rates to those clients on low incomes. The lowest end of your fee scale could even be free-of-charge work that you perform for charitable organizations, with the proportion of hours you spend on such work each month being necessarily limited for the good of the whole practice.

Some directly paying compensation systems dictate their own rates. From the accounting perspective it is easier to charge the agreed payable fee, although the recommended fee should be shown. Readers are recommended to use these considerations in conjunction with Appendix D.

4.9 Collecting revenue

There are two main aspects to collecting revenue from clients, namely invoicing them for work done and then ensuring that payment is made, as set out below.

4.9.1 Invoicing clients

Irrespective of what your fee schedule is, it is important to have a clear system for quoting for your services and for invoicing your clients. An invoice should be on your letterhead, unless you have specially-printed invoice stationery – in which case that should show all the details that your letterhead does. Invoices should include:

- the name and address of the recipient of your services;
- the client's employer and compensation claim number, if relevant;
- the type of service provided;

- the date(s) on which the service was provided;
- the charge rate;
- your relevant provider and registration numbers, where relevant;
- terms of payment, e.g., '7 days net' or 'Payment in 14 days required'.

For counselling practices, where the client pays, it is best to produce an invoice immediately after the session, for immediate settlement. One of the models that you may imitate is a classical medical practice, where a receptionist completes the service transaction by providing clients with their invoice and a receipt at the same time. A receipt can be in the form of a stamp on the invoice with the words 'PAID', including date, receptionist's signature and the method of settling the invoice.

Some practitioners choose to request payment in advance of the counselling session, so that the last transaction with the client is not of a financial nature. This may have some validity if the practitioner is acting as a receptionist as well as a service provider. If you wish to introduce such a system, the client needs to have been informed and accepted such a proposition, given that it is unconventional to seek full payment for any item or service prior to its delivery.

In your invoicing system you will need to establish a policy as to when payment is expected. Some clients may expect to take the invoice away and settle it later; some may prefer to pay by cheque rather than cash; and others may prefer to use credit cards. If you would like to provide credit-card facilities, you will need to contact a relevant bank and/or other credit provider. They will provide you with the vendor's equipment and instructions. You should expect to be charged for each transaction where the credit-card facility is used and, in some cases, establishment fees apply.

For compensation clients, your invoices should be forwarded to the relevant authority. You may choose to send your invoices immediately after the services have been provided, or to accumulate the charges and bill them on a monthly basis. Similarly, if your client is a corporate or government organization, it is reasonable to produce invoices on a monthly basis or as guided by your contract agreement with the organization. Your services might consist of managing a long-term change-management project, an employee stress analysis or the provision of a series of training seminars. In such an arrangement, the payment is usually expected on completion of agreed milestones or the entire project.

When you sign a contract for a longer-term project, you need to be sure that your finances can withstand the pressure of working for a number of weeks – or even months – without receiving any income, while possibly incurring salary and travel costs. There is also a gap between sending your invoice and receiving payment, which could be a minimum of 14 days and quite possibly 30 days or even longer. This is the distinct and very real problem of financial liquidity – see below.

4.9.2 Collecting and managing debt

If you allow clients to pay some time after invoices have been issued, you extend credit to them. In accounting terms they become your debtors. If you have any outstanding debt, it must be systematically managed because it affects your business cash flow, which is the bloodline of the practice.

The first step in debt management is to count the outstanding amount at least once a month. One simple, manual way of achieving this is to keep a sales journal that lists every client and the amount they owe. As each payment is received, that amount is deducted from the total amount owed by this client. At the end of each month, you can then determine the amount individually owed. If you use a computerized accounting system, it should automatically provide information on your debtors in categories defined by the period of outstanding debt, for instance: current (0–30 days), 31–60 days, 61–90 days and 91 days or more.

An effective debt-management system will ensure that the amounts owed for more than 90 days are a very small percentage of the overall debt. One approach is to issue 'statements' at the end of each month. Statements are very similar to invoices but they include the amounts due or overdue and the corresponding periods. Some businesses also attach a friendly reminder on the statement courteously requesting prompt payment of overdue amounts.

If issuing statements does not bring the desired result, the next step is usually to employ a debt-collection agency, which will take up the matter on your behalf (in return for a fee), initially by writing a stern letter requesting immediate payment and reminding your client that prompt payment will prevent legal costs. Another approach is to follow up all unpaid accounts by telephone, an activity preferably performed by someone other than the professional practitioner. A duplicate invoice or statement can then be issued if the client has 'lost' the original invoice.

If none of the above approaches produces a result, you may have to consider writing the owed amount off as a 'bad debt'. If you are reasonably certain that you will not recover some payments, it is best to discuss them with your accountant and act on his or her advice. It is a sobering thought that, unless you receive payment for the services that have been charged, there may be circumstances in which you may have to pay tax on this income even though it has not been received.

For psychologists providing individual counselling services, the issue of billing for non-attendance sometimes arises. It is possible to issue an invoice to the client who has not attended a session but did not cancel the appointment within the agreed period. This action is reasonable only if you have clearly informed the client of your policy on payment and non-attendance. It assumes that you have issued the client with a clear statement of your expectations and the rules for cancelling appointments, which the client has read and whose understanding you have checked. Such a statement could form part of your overall policy on payment. Once you have issued an invoice for non-attendance, you can pursue its payment in the same way as any other debt.

4.10 Accounting systems

Systematic debt management relies on accounting systems. Irrespective of how large your practice is, you will need to consider its accounting requirements. In a small practice, it may be possible to keep manual records and present them to an external accountant on a regular basis, for example quarterly.

In order to prepare your taxation-return documents, your accountant will need at least the following:

- bank statements;
- cheque stubs;
- bank paying-in books/counterfoils;
- issued invoices and/or your sales journal;
- receipt books;
- bills/invoices received from your suppliers;
- the petty cash book.

If you choose to maintain bookkeeping manually, the two most useful records are the cash book and the sales journal. These will provide you with a valuable picture of your business performance and are worth maintaining for your own information, not just to satisfy your accountant or tax inspector.

The cash book is divided into two sections, for payments and receipts respectively. Each entry corresponds to one transaction of any amount being paid or received. The payments section can be divided into various expenditure categories (or accounts), such as rent, wages, postage, etc. Table 4.1 overleaf shows an example of a cash-book entry.

The sales journal consists of a record of each invoice issued against each client. It can be further split into 'cash' and 'credit' groupings. It is helpful to note that the cash book contains entries relating to actual

Table 4.1: A sample cash book entry

| Date | Detail of transactions | Cheque/Receipt No. | PAYMENTS | | | | | | RECEIPTS | | | Bank balance (£) |
			Advertising (£)	Insurance (£)	Printing (£)	Telephone (£)	Wages (£)	Cash (£)	Credit (£)		
											1000
01/11/01	ABC Printing	101			150					850
02/11/01	A Receptionist	369					550			300
03/11/01	Mr Client	999						100		400

Table 4.2: Sales journal sample format

Invoice date	Client name	Client details	Invoice no.	Invoice amount	Date paid	Amount paid

money received and paid, while the sales journal contains the amounts invoiced. If you do not manage your debt effectively, the sales journal will show large amounts while the cash book will show little cash actually being received. See Table 4.2 for an example of a sales-journal entry.

If you find the maintenance of such accounting systems time-consuming and uninspiring, you need to delegate this responsibility to someone with the required vocational interest and skills. You, however, must still be in control of your practice, and so it is important to delegate rather than relinquish your responsibility for this important function. One way of ensuring that you stay in touch with the financial performance of your practice is to have a monthly briefing with your bookkeeper, who may then present you with the key monthly indicators such as:

- income from professional fees;
- total expenditure;
- profit (loss);
- amount of outstanding debt (e.g., in the category of 60 days plus).

If you would like to see these functions performed efficiently and have the advantage of regular financial reports, you will need to consider computerizing your accounting system.

4.11 Information systems

Over the last few decades, computers have changed the way businesses operate. The real information explosion of the late twentieth century has made computer technology accessible even to the smallest of businesses. They are no longer the domain of the largest and most prosperous companies. The word 'computer' has become synonymous with the microcomputer or personal computer, and this is what is meant here by this word, to distinguish it from the mainframe computers that are usually found in large organizations.

It is difficult to imagine a professional psychology practice operating efficiently nowadays without some assistance from computers. In fact, it will be increasingly more difficult to stay abreast of professional development without recourse to computer technology, with some conference proceedings, research papers and other of the most up-to-date information being available only via computers.

In your practice, you will either use a computer yourself or delegate the function to someone else. Whichever is your preferred behaviour, it is imperative to be at least aware of how a computer can assist in running your practice. This section is not meant to provide you with a detailed exposé of how computers work, but to describe briefly how they can make a positive impact on your practice. If you would like to learn further from other psychologists' experience with computers and about their application to private practice, you will benefit from joining a local computer-interest group, and/or joining the Mathematical, Statistical and Computing Section of the British Psychological Society.

Computer systems, in the most general of terms, consist of the machinery (the hardware) and the program instructions (the software). Your practice will gain no benefit from computer hardware unless appropriate software comes with it. To complete the system, you must add people – the users (and maybe programmers), who need lots of patience and training to achieve what you really want from the computer system.

4.11.1 Software

Most popular software is nowadays bundled together with the hardware. This means that you can obtain at the time of your initial computer purchase, and thus very cost-efficiently, some of the standard programs on the market today – amounting to probably half of your practice software needs. Other programs can be purchased separately and are available in specialist computer stores, through various catalogues, or directly from the distributor via postal supply or Internet download.

If your identified computer needs cannot be met by generally available software, you may consider contracting a programmer to custom-design a solution for your practice. While this will almost always be a more expensive option, its flexibility can outweigh the extra expense.

Whatever way you choose to purchase your software, you need to account for its costs in your initial computer budget. When you obtain quotes for computer hardware, you should also check the availability and cost of software. As an estimate, it is quite common for all the software to cost a significant proportion of the whole of the computer set-up costs. If your needs include computer-based psychological testing or powerful statistical analyses, this amount could increase – although the budget-conscious user will appreciate that basic statistics may be readily obtained on a conventional spreadsheet.

If you plan to operate a number of computers in your practice, you might need to purchase separate software packages for each, as most of them have a licence to operate on only one computer at any one time. Readers are strongly cautioned against pirated and illegally copied programs. Software is intellectual property that must be legitimately purchased, for its authors deserve their royalty recompense –

and you do not want to end up in jail or with a hefty fine (not to mention the stain on your reputation).

The software that is likely to be used by professional psychology practices can be divided into the categories that are discussed in more detail below.

Word processing

The most basic use of computers in every psychology practice is for word processing the reports, letters, invoices and all other varieties of written communication that the practice needs. The most popular word-processing packages appear to be Microsoft's Word and Word-Perfect. Computers have well and truly taken over this area of administration, mainly because of the significant flexibility of editing and correcting errors (and the high quality of printing through ink-jet and laser printers).

If your computers are used only for the word-processing function, they become very expensive typewriters. Such a scenario is somewhat parallel to owning a Porsche, only to drive it to a local shop around the corner. The power of today's personal computers enables them to deliver far more productivity and efficiency to your practice, if you only care to explore further. The use of mailing lists, databases, and presentations are three examples.

Spreadsheets

A relative newcomer into the English vocabulary is the word 'spreadsheet'. It describes a special kind of software that looks like an electronic page divided into rows and columns. Its main purpose is to perform calculations of mathematical, financial, statistical or any other numerical nature. Essentially it is a very sophisticated calculator, which enables any user to become a programmer.

Before the arrival of spreadsheets on personal computers, all computer programming had to be performed using special computer languages. In contrast, by using simple formulae and English-like expressions it is possible to create spreadsheet-based programs that can be used as many times as needed to determine some of the most complex (or most simple) answers to numerical calculations. The most popular spreadsheet programs currently are Microsoft's Excel and Lotus 1-2-3.

Its most useful applications in private psychology practice will be in the area of financial and statistical analysis. Its sophistication and ease of use will enable you to apply spreadsheets for a variety of functions – for example, your initial break-even analysis before commencing your practice, and then the ongoing cash-flow analysis that on a monthly basis will determine how much money you need to have in the bank to meet all your expenditure commitments. Or one might wish to run an algorithm on estimating income based on the assumption that a drop in fees will produce more clients, where the various combinations of percentage fee drop, extra clients and economies of scale may be calculated quite readily. Although it is possible to do all these analyses using just a calculator, the electronic spreadsheet increases your efficiency in this area and frees up time to be spent on more productive activities. The electronic method also preserves a record of your basic data as well as your conclusions.

Databases

'Database' is another word introduced into the English language by the computer age. It can be thought of as a three-dimensional spread-sheet. Databases are extremely useful tools for holding, organizing and reporting information about entities with multiple components, such as clients, staff, assets, books and so on. The information relating to such entities is usually made up of many items, such as surname, date of birth, date of first visit, book title and so on, and referred to as 'fields'.

Another analogy that may help in understanding the application of databases is the working of a filing cabinet. Database software pro-vides most efficient solutions for problems that otherwise can only be painstakingly solved by filing lots of information in files, which are then grouped into cabinet drawers, which are then grouped into filing cabinets, which are then stored in rooms, etc. To hold lots of data in one computer in such a way that its contents can be relatively easily analysed is the advantage brought by databases.

The application of database software will depend on your capabil-ity to operate it, and your interest in computer solutions. It is, like spreadsheets, another relatively easy-to-use program tool to help you run your business. If you choose to create your own database solu-tions, it will probably be most productive to select one out of many excellent products on the market and become proficient in that one package. The level of sophistication and power in such packages has increased markedly in recent years at the expense of greater complex-ity and programming difficulty. Fortunately, at the same time, many other data-based products have been specifically designed for tasks that previously had to be programmed by users.

One example is a database of clients for marketing purposes. Rather than having to develop a customized solution for your practice, a number of relatively inexpensive software packages are readily avail-able for the task of organizing information about clients. There are also other database-type products specifically designed for professional pri-vate practice, and you will be well advised to consider these during the establishment of your practice. They contain computerized solutions to managing information about clients, services provided to the clients, and some aspects of financial management such as invoicing and reconciliation of receipts. Some of them have been developed with the specific purpose of servicing a professional *psychology* practice, while others are more generally applicable to any type of private practice.

Databases may be interrogated as part of practice management. An analysis of sources of referrals, ease of fee collection, and even the effectiveness of types of treatment may be analysed. The practice manager will want to know about signals for action, effective outcomes, payments, and warning signs. Formulating questions important to the practice is the first stage – and the answers to those sorts of questions are most readily obtainable by interrogating a practice's client database.

One of the things that practitioners discover is the need for good data collection. To this end, the types and extent of information, as well as its security, should be under constant review.

Accounting packages

While certain office administration packages developed for private practices contain some financial management information, none of these can completely replace a professional accounting package. Accounting software is usually general-purpose in function and can be purchased in any software or office-stationery store. There are many different packages available, and the best approach for selecting one is to base your judgement on its user-friendliness and its ability to produce the financial reports that can be effectively used in managing your business.

Although there have been hundreds of accounting software packages on sale over recent years, only a handful have become very popular. It would appear that such popularity would not have been possible without some simple design features. Some examples are: Sage-Tetra, Quicken, and Tass Books. You should not find it difficult to locate someone in business who uses one of these packages and learn from their experience.

The most common elements found in most accounting packages are the following four:

- Accounts Payable;
- Accounts Receivable;
- General Ledger;
- Cash Book.

As an addition, extra modules such as Payroll may be available to add to the system. The greatest benefit from maintaining an in-house software accounting system is that on a regular and frequent basis you can peruse financial reports that provide a snapshot of the health of your business. Such reports will include your profit and loss statement, and balance sheet.

Presentation software

There is a variety of software available with the specific purpose of generating audio-visual presentation materials. If your practice involves presenting seminars, talks or lectures, the quality of your presentation materials, such as slides, can be greatly enhanced by such software packages. They are also likely to save a considerable amount of preparation time. Some packages now include multimedia functionality, which means that you can embed voice, video clips, and still or moving graphics as part of your presentation.

Some of the most popular presentation software includes Microsoft PowerPoint (which is included in the Microsoft Office Professional package), Harvard Graphics and CorelDraw. Once you have generated images using this software, you can project the images directly onto a large screen from your computer, or have them printed as overhead projector acetates or 35mm slides.

Graphics packages

Graphics packages enable you to create some of the most complex images with the greatest of ease and enjoyment. You need, however, some skills and creativity to use the packages effectively.

Apart from generating elements of your brochures or other material for distribution to your clients, it is unlikely that you will use this type of package. As a general rule, since psychologists are not vocationally aligned with artists, this type of activity is left to more efficient and productive experts.

Desktop publishing

The packages described as desktop publishing are special kinds of software combining word processing and graphics. They provide the user with a tool to generate a more sophisticated layout for documents that have already been word-processed and to add any other graphics, tables or graphs. Examples are Adobe Pagemaker and Quark Express.

Unless your practice is involved in the creation of book-quality documents, it is likely that the latest releases of word-processing packages will be more than adequate for most of your document work. A growing sophistication of simple publishing software (such as Microsoft Publisher) makes it easy nowadays to produce high-quality brochures and publications with minimum effort.

Statistical analysis

Another application of computer software for psychology is statistical analysis (over and above what database software can do). If your psychology product involves designing and administering surveys, you will need an efficient tool for analysing the results and presenting reports. If the surveys are of limited quantity and scope, it may be quite sufficient to use spreadsheet or database software. Indeed, most popularly available spreadsheets have built-in sophisticated statistical functions for this purpose. Their capacity for graphical presentation and printing, either in combination with word-processing software or within spreadsheets, is also more than adequate for most of the presentations you will require.

If your practice's requirements to conduct survey analyses extend beyond the spreadsheet capacity, you may wish to consider packages that are specifically designed for the purpose of statistical analysis, such as SPSSx or Minitab.

Communications
The last category of software applicable to the psychology private practice is generally referred to as 'communications'. It enables computers to connect to each other via telephone cables and modems. For computers to exchange information, a special program is required to control the process of such interchange. The application for such programs extends to Internet connection, electronic banking, email, computer faxes, or simple data interchange between two computers. Because of the recent explosion of interest in the Internet, most of the communications software that you will probably need is nowadays sold packaged up with computer hardware or given free by the Internet Service Providers.

4.11.2 Hardware

The choice of a computer hardware system (generally with standard software packages included in the price) is often shrouded in mystery, although it is no different from purchasing any other piece of machinery, which has to provide for the user, at an optimum cost, what is expected from it. One of the mistakes you can make is to select one on price alone. You would not do this with a house, for example, or any other large purchase. So, before you start comparing prices, you should determine your needs and identify the criteria on the basis of which you will make your selection of computer hardware.

The first question that any computer salesperson will ask you is 'What will you use it for?' If you are unsure, look through the categories of computer software just discussed. You will then need to determine what proportion of time your computer will be used for in each of those areas of activity. For example, if it is mostly going to be used for word processing and very little for accounting and testing, you will not need the speed normally required for fast calculations in financial and statistical analyses. In other words, your needs for software will define your hardware needs. There is no point in purchasing a computer that does not perform well for the software you need. Software actually drives your hardware needs.

You need to be aware that programs continue to evolve, and with their constant enhancement they require more from hardware: more memory, more disk space, or a faster processing speed. Keeping this in mind, it may be a costly error to purchase a superseded computer model merely because of the attractiveness of its price. While this may form a reasonable decision when purchasing a car, because it is still likely to meet your expectations for driving you around in many years' time, it may not be the case with your computer. Unfortunately, depreciation on computer systems is so steep that in two or three years it may be difficult to give your computer away, let alone sell it.

One of the first choices you will need to make is between Apple Macintosh or IBM-compatible technology, although there is less and less difference between the two technologies as far as the user is concerned. Depending on which area of practice you specialize in, it may be an important factor for your computer systems to be compatible with your corporate clients.

One of the barriers to overcome in purchasing computer hardware is the jargon that salespeople tend to use – sometimes to extend their control over unsuspecting newcomers into the field. It therefore pays to do some research before committing yourself to a particular purchase. There are a few basic facts about computer hardware that may be of some assistance when making your selection. Relevant background information is set out next.

Computer systems are made of the following components:

- central processing unit;
- random access memory;
- disk storage;
- monitors;
- printers.

Each of these components is described further below.

Central processing unit

The central processing unit (CPU) is the heart of any computer; its architecture is expressed in 'bits' (e.g., 16-bit, 32-bit), which represent the way computers handle information for its processing. All CPUs also have clocks that dictate the speed of their information processing; clock speed is measured in megahertz (MHz). The faster the CPU speed the faster the computer will operate. So, in general, it is safest to select the largest and the fastest CPU currently available on the market – currently an Intel Pentium III processor or equivalent.

Even so, what you buy is likely to be superseded within a few months of your purchase – processing power tends to double every 18 months or so. And in addition the software developers regularly release enhanced versions of the standard software, which will demand more disk space and memory, and so the cycle continues. By buying the latest hardware for your price range, at least you will be as up-to-date as you can manage.

Random access memory

Random access memory (RAM) is the place where most of the information processing takes place when computers are in operation. It is a temporary area and its size determines the amount of information that can be worked on at any one time. RAM is measured in megabytes (MB) and one megabyte can store one million bytes (or characters) of information.

The more memory the better, because it will allow your software to run faster, and some popular programs described earlier now recommend at least 16 MB of RAM to run efficiently. Purchasing a computer with more RAM than the standard offer will generally assure your system of better performance and longer durability. You will need at least 32 MB RAM to run multimedia and CDs effectively – but most personal computers today offer at least twice that amount.

Disk storage

A 'hard disk' is the device in which the information is stored for the longer term in your computer and from which all programs are imported into RAM when you switch on your computer. Because the software, as it becomes more sophisticated, also becomes more voluminous, there is likely to be a growing need for larger hard-disk capacities. The new standard is likely to be 4 Gigabyte (4000 MB) and if you must settle for any less, it should not be much less.

'Floppy disks' or 'diskettes' are flexible storage units that are currently 3.5 inches square in size and 1.44 MB in storage capacity. They are separate from the computer itself and are read from/written to by insertion into a diskette drive, which forms part of the hardware you buy with a computer system. One such drive is required as a minimum, so as to be able to copy programs from diskettes onto the hard disk and also so as to provide a back-up facility for files resident on the hard disk.

CD-ROMs are compact disks with read-only memory. They have a greater capacity for storage than diskettes and, because of this, CD-ROM technology is increasingly being used where large amounts of data need to be held. Examples are telephone directories, reference works, and collections of research documents. Software is also distributed using this medium rather than multiple diskettes. CD-ROM drives are usually sold as part of the hardware package in conjunction with multimedia kits, including stereo sound cards and speakers. More recently, CD writers are available which can be used to record an enormous amount of data on to CDs. When there is a need for back-up of large amounts of data, zip drives may be considered.

Monitors

Monitors display information to the user. They are also referred to by their more old-fashioned name of 'visual display units' (VDUs) or just 'screens'. The two main considerations with VDU purchase are 'resolution' and colour. 'Resolution' represents the number of pixels (dots) comprising the image on the screen: the higher the resolution, the clearer the image. Resolution is expressed as the number of horizontal pixels by the number of vertical pixels on the screen (e.g., 800x600). Colour monitors also have ranges of colours available, and the higher-resolution monitors have many more colours available, measured in the thousands. Most high-quality software demands a range of colours.

Printers

Printers are vital items of equipment that will determine the quality of all the output produced by your computer. Currently the three most popular types of printer available on the market are termed dot-matrix, inkjet, and laser. Printer performance is compared largely by speed of throughput, measured in pages per minute (e.g., 8 ppm), and dot resolution of character image, measured in dots per inch (e.g., 600 dpi).

Dot-matrix printers are of the lowest quality and should only be considered for drafts or purely internal documents (such as accounting reports or work schedules). Inkjets spray ink onto the paper through nozzles in order to produce dots forming the characters, and this type is the second-best quality of printer. Laser printers provide the highest and most consistent quality of output. It is recommended that laser printers be considered as a standard for any business purporting to provide quality professional services.

Colour versions of the latter are also available; however, the cost of high-quality laser colour printers is still high, although it is likely that they will become standard in the foreseeable future. The currently available colour inkjet printers provide reasonable colour quality, but they tend to create a compromise in normal black printing quality and printing speed. Colour also increases the cost of the printing of each page.

The whole system

When you have chosen the computer package that you believe will meet your needs (current typical price £1000–£2000 per desktop computer system), you should also consider post-purchase support and warranty offered by the retailer, or make your own arrangements with a computer maintenance firm. A maintenance contract can be more valuable than the short-term saving on the total price, given the costs of repairs and replacements. Remember, too, in negotiation that buying your software and hardware from the same place is an excellent opportunity to get substantial discounts, because add-ons are generally cheaper.

Whatever you buy, make sure you get the appropriate diskettes and manuals for the built-in software (although you should bear in mind that some help manuals are nowadays screen-based and built into the software package). The source material is not only valuable but also an indication of genuine ownership.

4.11.3 Research and communication via the Internet

The word 'Internet' has been propelled out of its past university-based obscurity into prominence in the last decade. Its impact on business is at this stage uncertain and has probably been overstated. Nevertheless, there is little doubt that the impact of electronic communication will continue to increase in almost every area of our lives, business included. Rather than explaining the Internet, which has been the subject of many informative books (e.g., Kent, 1994), its application to psychology practice will be discussed here in two main areas: research and communication.

The Internet is essentially a collection of computer networks around the world. It is maintained by an array of satellite links, computer cables and numerous telephone connections. Through this network, it is possible to gain access to a vast number of databases containing valuable information, and to communicate with millions of other individuals.

To gain access to the Internet, you need to contact one of the many Internet Service Providers (ISPs), and it pays to compare their prices. They will usually provide you with all the software you need to communicate with their central computer. You will also need a modem connected to your computer in order to do that. The retailers of modems may include a free trial period of connection to a particular ISP, which is a very cost-efficient way to try and see if it has some appeal for you. Along with a possible one-off account-establishment fee (many do not charge), most ISPs charge for the connection on an hourly basis as you use the service – although there are now some free services where the cost of the service is borne by revenue from the advertising that appears on screen, and the only cost to you would be the telephone line charges.

At the lowest level, communication can take place by a simple email connection which your Internet Service Provider will make available as part of the normal access for a small fee. Using email is equivalent to electronic faxing or writing to someone – you need to know who the addressee is. It is simply another written form of communication but it is extremely fast and inexpensive. Because the connection to your ISP's computer is usually at local rates, if you are located in a metropolitan area it means that international email costs you no more than a local call – a few minutes' connection to the computer which, if you are doing all of your transmissions at once, amounts to very little.

Two other types of electronic communication are 'newsgroups' and 'bulletin boards'. These provide an opportunity to relate to people of similar interest and exchange views on various subjects with vast numbers of people at the same time. There are many such newsgroups designed by and for psychologists working in specific professional areas around the world.

One of the most popular parts of the Internet is the World Wide Web (www). This is a network of computer sites containing all kinds of documents consisting of text and/or images. Through your Internet access program, known as a 'browser', you can find numerous documents that other people have placed for you to read. Anyone can place information on his or her ISP's computer, which forms a website that anyone else in the world can 'visit' or 'browse'. There are many websites of interest to psychologists which enable further opportunity for useful information exchange.

Three cautions need to be made about information on websites. One is that there is no guarantee of the provenance and integrity of the information made accessible; the second is to be alert to giving private information; and the third is to beware of contracting electronic viruses.

As an Internet user, you will be able to establish your own website 'home page' on which you can publish your articles or inform others about any subject you might be interested in. This is the area of interest to most businesses that can see it as an opportunity to advertise and market their products (see section 4.7.7). For psychologists, the whole Internet experience can provide a great opportunity to network with others and exchange ideas, thus reducing the feeling of isolation in private practice. At the same time, it can provide an extremely efficient tool for researching a particular topic of professional interest and for keeping oneself abreast of the latest information in the world without spending any time away from the practice.

Information placed on the Internet by universities and other organizations may provide a reasonable starting point for researching a particular topic of interest. You can also perform comprehensive literature searches via computer-linked library resources for which there may be extra charges. In this case, you can use the Internet as a gateway into the desired library of abstract resources (see also Wallace, 1999).

4.11.4 Computer administration

There are some essential tasks you need to undertake to ensure that your computer investment serves you well. Computers are just machines, and as such they are fallible. Disks crash, files get corrupted, and viruses get transmitted. It is best to avoid problems by conducting regular back-ups and checks of your system. Backing up your computer hard disk is probably one of the most important functions that will prevent small problems becoming potential business disasters.

There are some simple rules to follow when creating a back-up of your work:

- Always keep at least two back-up copies, usually the latest and second-latest versions. In that way, if a crash occurs during your backing-up, you will still have one good copy.
- Always back up your data (documents, accounts, test results, etc.) *daily*. These items of information are most vulnerable because they will be either irreplaceable or very costly to reproduce.
- The purchased software can always be reloaded from the original diskettes (or their copies).
- Always keep at least one back-up disk off the premises where the computer system exists. Storing a back-up with the computer is as bad as not having a back-up at all in cases of burglary or fire.

To sharpen your thinking and commitment to keeping effective back-ups, imagine that the next day when you come into your practice the computer is gone. Then ask yourself how quickly can you restore the entire system on a new machine.

It is also prudent to check your system regularly for viruses and other possible problems, and always check other people's floppy disks before loading them onto your system. There are a number of effective virus-checking software packages available (e.g., from Norton or McAfee). Some Internet Service Providers offer a virus checker, which is easily downloaded from the Web.

One way to ensure that computer administration tasks are done regularly and thoroughly is to delegate them to an expert, who spends a few hours every month keeping your system in perfect health.

4.12 Psychometric tests

One of the most distinctive things that a psychologist does is to use psychometric tests. Appropriate skills in administering, scoring and interpreting such tests are dealt with to some extent within formal courses. The number of tests in the marketplace has risen dramatically, and getting it wrong can be costly both in financial terms and in terms of your professional reputation.

In response to an enquiry, the Help Desk at the British Psychological Society will send out a package of material on behalf of the Steering Committee on Test Standards (*Psychological Testing: a User's Guide*, 1995). A leaflet on frequently asked questions (FAQ) will also be enclosed. The authors are not, however, aware of any official or approved list of psychometric suppliers, although a non-evaluative list is available from the British Psychological Society. It is probably better for practitioners to keep their own database on test suppliers. To do this there are two good places to start. One is to look at test manuals themselves, which indicate the supplier, and a department or colleague owning a test is likely to be willing to provide details; the second way is to look at the comprehensive BPS test reviews (see Bartram, 1997, for example). Such reviews include a supplementary list of the organizations that supplied the reviewed tests.

Psychologists may consider being assessed for a BPS Certificate of Competence in Occupational Testing. On request, psychologists may receive an information pack on becoming a Level A and/or a Level B test user. Level B extends on Level A. The information packs are both headed 'Certificate and Register of Competence in Occupational Testing'. Attention is drawn to two full-length independent reviews of test instruments currently in use. These are not reviews in the more common sense of being a relatively brief written evaluation. Rather, they are both a textbook and a reference work. The review edited by Bartram (1997) deals with Ability and Aptitude Tests (Level A). A second edition of the *Review of Personality Assessment Instruments* (Level B) was published in 2001 (edited by P. A. Lindley). Furthermore, you should be aware of an Open Learning Program for Level A candidates (see Bartram and Lindley, 2000).

An increasing number of psychological tests have become available in 'soft' computer format in addition to the traditional 'hard' paper and pencil style. Even more tests provide the option of computerized scoring. The tests can be either administered personally (to individuals or to groups) and then scored at the practice using specially purchased software or sent to an agency providing scoring services. The latter usually takes a little longer but reduces the need for computer investment in-house.

If your psychology practice involves frequent testing, you may consider providing a computer terminal for your clients to access. You will also need to invest in the testing software that is usually sold on the basis of the number of times it is used – that is, per client (not unlike the paper-based materials). This relatively new form of administering psychological tests generates attendant cautions. The usual strictures apply just as much to this form of testing as applies to conventional testing. There are also BPS *Guidelines for the Development and Use of Computer Based Assessments* (1999). And the BPS booklet entitled *Psychological Testing: A User's Guide* (1995) covers the issues of:

- what to look for in a psychological test;
- what qualifies as competence in the use of psychological tests;
- a commitment to responsible use of tests.

One of the problematic areas here is what exactly is a psychological test, as distinct from other forms of test. Why should some tests be restricted to psychologists' use and some not? Among the issues to consider are the empirical base of the test, properly derived norms, a body of supporting research, and the need for psychological skills in both administering and scoring/interpreting. A really important issue is that no matter how a test is labelled, there are guiding principles about its use. It is to these principles that psychologists should adhere. The Levels A and B programmes are an excellent way of ensuring an understanding of those principles, and in gaining skills in test usage.

4.13 Developing practice excellence

Businesses go through a life cycle of identifiable phases from infancy and growth, through mid-career and maturity, to decline. Each phase can last for a variable period of time, and it is not easy to predict its duration. It is useful to recognize the phase that your practice is in and behave accordingly, to assure it of corporate longevity. It will help, too, if you develop practice excellence in the major aspects of its operation.

If you have already established your practice, following the principles outlined in the last chapter, you have entered the initial stage. This phase is likely to be quite exciting and demanding of your time and energy. In the business-infancy stage you will probably be willing to invest both of these in large measure, in the hope that your life will in fact be better for it. As time goes on, you will inevitably discover that the demands that the practice places on your time continue to increase, and that you cannot easily control the growth of your practice.

The frustrating part of it all will be that, despite your working harder than ever before, you are actually making less money. The whole experience of gaining income from your practice may become very uncertain and unpredictable. When you reach the point of feeling tired of trying to make it succeed, and the need for a holiday from it all becomes an obsessive thought, it is time to stand back and take a serious look at the way in which you run your practice. If you have never reached this point, it may be because you have been able to take serious looks at your business regularly throughout its development. At those times you might have discovered that the only way to retain your sanity and enjoy the challenge of generating your own income from your efforts is to start thinking of your practice as a system.

A Barclays Bank report (1999) noted that '... for the third year running the survival rates of small businesses have improved ... the proportion of small businesses surviving past their third year of trading increased to 52.5% [in April 1999], compared to 49.6% in April 1997'. Part of this improvement in success rate has to be attributed to the improvement of planning, thought, and commitment to success – in other words, practice excellence.

4.13.1 *Developing business systems*

In his very readable management book, Gerber (1995) proposed a new paradigm to enable a business to produce the desired outcomes for life. Gerber's proposition is to think of the business itself as a product, so that it can be franchised. The franchise model means that your practice could be conducted by anyone else who chose to purchase it from you.

There are possibly some limitations to this paradigm in its application to professional practices that have intense person-to-person interaction inbuilt. If your business is totally dependent on you and cannot function without you, then it really is no business at all. It has become your life and it will probably control you rather than you using it to achieve your life's principal goals.

If, on the other hand, your business is to function independently of you as a system, it needs to have predictable components and it needs to deliver consistently high-quality products to its customers. Applying the franchise paradigm to your thinking about your practice will lead you to design it in such a way that your clients will be able to expect and receive service of the same quality every time. When they tell others about you, that same expectation about what and how you deliver your services will be met.

This transition of your practice into a predictable system of service delivery can be thought of as a phase of 'getting organized'. While you may be providing quality services to your customers at the moment, check whether it is happening by accident or by design. Let us explore some questions to help you define the extent to which your practice is organized as a system.

- Do all your clients hear the same greeting when they phone you?
- If you are not available, are all clients given clear alternatives as to how to establish contact with you?
- Are all your clients given the same (and clear) explanation as to what to expect in the way of professional services?
- Are all your clients greeted when they come to see you and looked after in the same way every time?
- Are all your clients able to make appointments with you when they need to, and are they all provided with a card identifying the date and time of next appointment?
- Are all your clients billed for the services in the same way, given invoices and receipts in a consistent format, and offered the same payment options?
- Are all your suppliers' bills paid within their specified credit terms?
- Do all your staff know what your expectations are of their performance?
- Do all your staff receive their pay at the same time and on a regular basis?
- Is the same level of courtesy extended to all of your stakeholders?
- Are correspondence and requests dealt with promptly?

The overriding question here is whether your clients can have the assurance that they will receive the same level of service every time they make contact with your practice. In stepping back and taking a look at your business, you need to view it from your client's point of view.

4.13.2 *Being customer-focused*

To be able to appraise your practice from your client's perspective, you need first to identify who your client is exactly. In the psychology business, quite often beyond the primary individual clients are secondary clients or client organizations that actually pay for your services. Examples are compensation systems, or employers who pay for your services delivered to their claimants or employees.

It is worthwhile to re-emphasize here that the identification of your client is crucial. Are you primarily responsible to the person across the desk, the organization that commissioned you, the person who pays the bill, or those who receive your report? For a fuller discussion of 'Who is the client?' see Francis and Cameron (1997).

One example scenario for an organizational psychologist is where a human resources department of a company is funding a project involving numerous other clients – managers and supervisors, team members of work groups, and others. Your services to each of these groups of clients are important, although only one of them will transact the payment for your business. Other hidden clients in an organizational setting are the superiors of those who have contracted your services, such as the board of directors, although you may never meet them face to face. There are also other individuals or groups who are decision makers regarding the referral of the individual clients to your practice. They form your indirect clients who also, nevertheless, need to be considered when you become customer-focused.

At this point of your business, namely 'becoming organized', you need to identify the expectations of all types of your clients and ensure that the way your business meets their expectations is professional and consistent. This assumes that your value system contains a certain commitment to excellence in all of your practice's endeavours, but particularly in relation to your clients' expectations. You may have had experiences where you as a customer were impressed by the level of commitment given to quality, or you might remember situations where the opposite took place. It would be worthwhile to analyse each of those experiences in every shop, hotel or solicitor's office you have visited. How did you feel as a customer? What specific experiences made you feel like returning to the same service provider? Were your expectations met? Were you aware of any expectations you had prior to your contact with the service providers?

You will probably discover that the process of satisfying customers is mostly unconscious. The transactions that take place between the provider and the receiver are nevertheless quite powerful. How clients feel about the service they receive is far more important than what they process at the cognitive level. Their feelings about the whole transaction are often determined by the smallest detail that you may completely miss unless you begin looking at your business from your customers' viewpoints.

In a psychology practice all your clients – direct and indirect, primary, secondary and tertiary – must be considered as your customers. Each one of them has a potential to help your business succeed by referring others, returning for more of your services or contracting your services in a project.

4.13.3 Charting the customer-service process

Clients come in contact with you and your practice in many different ways. Your behaviour toward them will form a lasting impression that will impact on your business. To ensure that all points of contact with clients promote a positive image that encourages them to continue the client–provider relationship, the steps in the process where clients interact with the practice need first to be identified. One way to begin is to draw a line representing the clients' journey, along which they pass a number of points of contact with your practice, starting with an initial phone call, arriving at your premises, finding a car parking space, entering through the door, and so on. At each point they experience feelings related to their interaction with your practice.

Follow this journey with them, in their steps, and list all sorts of little details that could make big impacts on their experience. At each point of contact there are events that can be controlled by your business system: how the client is greeted, what options are given at the reception to the person, how their questions are answered. All the examples of such events that can be identified should be, and should be presented as a chart of activities. Such a chart will show who is responsible for which activity and how one activity is connected with another. Some of them will show a number of options leading to a few activities, depending on the preceding scenarios.

This customer-service process chart will be easily recognized by the organizational practitioners who assist their client organizations to achieve better performance and continuous improvement in their processes. There is no reason why the same change-intervention tool should not be applied to another organization – your practice. The teaching of applied psychology provides a solid basis upon which to create practice systems that aim for excellence. And such generic – but possibly dormant – skills are available for the process of running a business. Your underlying technical knowledge of human behaviour, and its biological basis, can be put to good use in becoming a change agent within your own practice.

4.13.4 Improving the customer-service process

Set out in this section are some specific comments on the likely steps on the customer-service process chart that you need to have in place.

Initial contact
One of the small but vital details that can often make a big impact on the client's perception of quality of service is the experience of the first contact. This may take place through a phone call, a personal visit, or even a written request. How your practice is presented in that initial contact will remain in a client's perception with the power of a classical primacy effect.

To maximize the positive impact on a client, you need to develop a system for responding to new contacts. First, you will need to define the perception that you would like the new or potential client to form about your practice. For example, the condensed message you might like to communicate could be:

- We are caring.
- We are professional.
- We offer quality.

Whatever the message, you can develop systems to ensure that, at each point of contact with a client, this communication takes place effectively. It cannot be overemphasized that a discreet manner is vital in psychology. Talking loudly at reception, for example, can be acutely embarrassing to clients. The information they volunteer and the questions you pose should be inaudible to others.

In developing a system that will deliver your message, there is a need for innovation, documentation, implementation, training and monitoring. The results of monitoring will lead to further innovation, and so on. The system of delivering excellent service is a continuous process that must evolve to meet the changing needs of your clients. If, instead, the process of initial contacts with your clients is not systematized, it is left to chance – and randomness.

Your receptionist staff, your network, books and articles will all play a part in creating an innovative way to greet a client and to ask the right questions. For example, a greeting beginning with the words: 'How can we help you?' may lead to better results than simply 'Good morning'. When a client asks for an appointment with Psychologist X, the response may be: 'Have you seen Dr/Mr/Ms X before?', which may then lead to another selective response, or providing a handout, depending on the answer to the initial question.

A system only exists if it can be replicated with reasonable predictability, and this can only take place if the agreed innovation is documented in some form. It can be an instruction sheet to the receptionist, for example. Such an instrument can be used in a short training session and displayed in a prominent place in the office. If the system works well, and your regular receptionist is replaced by a temporary assistant, they will be able to follow the instructions quite easily. In a business system, there should be few surprises and few assumptions. If anything is left to chance, your inability to predict will not ensure a consistently high-quality experience.

Yet you cannot assume that operational procedures are followed simply because they are written down. Thus monitoring of a System of Initial Contact will involve some behavioural observation, measurement, and analysis. The overall practice system needs to include some counting and measuring. This is another area where a wide training in statistical and scientific methods of measurement should provide a valuable advantage for a psychologist in business.

Measurement of compliance with the procedures may include ongoing collection of data, regular surveys, random checks, or a combination of these and any other creative methodology. Their aim is to ensure that the written procedures are followed, as well as to provide some basis for evaluating the extent to which your innovations with client contact have been successful. By consistently collecting relevant data over a period of time, and experimenting with different greetings (for example), you will be able to determine trends that will tell you how effective your innovations are.

You can establish systems that really work for you, not by guessing but by documenting the system, providing staff training, testing the system in operation, and then refining it.

Information on entry

Another milestone in the life of a client–provider relationship is the moment of the first appointment during which some transaction takes place and service is provided. It is a significant moment of truth. For many clients, the appointment may be the very first time they have consulted a psychologist, and their experience may be loaded with uncertainty and anxiety.

The information that the client is given at the point of entry into your practice may reduce or heighten this state. In more homely terms, first impressions count a great deal. By applying a systematic innovation approach, you can determine the types of questions most clients wish they could have asked at the first interview but were afraid to. You can construct that list simply by talking to your clients, or talking to other psychologists and combining their intuitive knowledge.

Your system solution could be a reader-friendly handout that is given to clients on their first visit. The issues that are covered by such a handout may include:

- What is involved in a consulting session?
- How long will each session be?
- How many sessions will I need?
- How much will it cost me?
- How and when do I pay?
- Should I (or could I) bring my partner and/or my children?
- Will you use some psychological tests?
- What will be expected from me during the consulting process?
- Will I be given any homework to do between appointments?
- Will I be given any written reports about me?
- Will our discussion be confidential?
- Will you record our session using a tape or video recorder?
- What happens if I cannot come to my next appointment?

The handout addressing the above issues could be read by clients while waiting for their first session. There may be many other ways of reducing clients' initial anxiety, and of providing useful information to them at the same time. The approach suggested here is simply an example of applying innovation and systems to ensure that each client has a high-quality, positive experience with predictable consistency. The process of continuous innovation and its systematic application will lead to excellence in practice.

The formalities

Every practice should ensure that each client knows that the psychologist is registered to practise psychology (and the registration certificate should be on view), that the psychologist is governed by a Code of Professional Conduct. The psychologist is required to act at all times in a professional manner. Information about the formalities should be communicated to clients, as set out next.

In relation to *professional standards*:

- Clients may expect to receive the best psychological help available. This means that where the consulting professional does not have adequate expertise in a particular set of circumstances, a referral should be made.
- Clients should expect to be treated with courtesy and respect.
- Clients have the right to cease a consultation or the professional relationship at any time.

In relation to *information*:

- Clients have a right to information on themselves.
- Where clients are denied information about themselves, they are advised that there are legal avenues of redress.
- The practising psychologist owns the records on clients.
- Clients are encouraged to ask as many questions as they wish, and have a corresponding right to satisfactory answers.
- Any concerns expressed will be dealt with expeditiously and effectively.
- Where appropriate, an explanation will be given of how a psychologist differs from a psychiatrist.

In relation to *confidentiality*, confidences will be strictly kept except under certain specified conditions (such as a requirement to divulge to a court of law or disclosure with the client's permission).

On the matter of *participation*, if the client wishes another person to be present in consultations (such as an interpreter, a family member or another professional adviser), then that wish should be followed unless there are strong reasons not to do so. Clients should be expected to take an active part in their assessment and treatment (which also makes therapeutic intervention more effective). If you have a client-rights statement (see below), consider having it on display. Such an explicit expression of caring can only be beneficial.

The information transaction at the point of entry is two-way. Your system will probably require certain information about your clients regarding their demographics, source of referral and compensation status. A first-time client will need to complete a form, probably designed exclusively for your practice.

You may wish to determine the most acceptable means by which this information can be obtained while at the same time sending the desired message to the client about how you conduct your practice. For example, should it be a self-administered form or should a receptionist ask the questions and interact personally with the client at the same time? Unless you ask your receptionist and your clients some questions about how the process works now, you may never know how to improve it.

For an organizational psychologist, entry into an organization may mean something quite different from a client entering into a counselling/clinical practice. The relationship with the client organization may start with a visit to the organization's premises. The initial phase of the consulting process will be referred to as 'entry'. The principles of a service system apply to this scenario perhaps even more powerfully. Your behaviour at every step will demonstrate your practice's commitment to excellence. The consistency of this behaviour is just as important in shaping the client's perception of you as a service provider and influencing their experiences.

By providing a brief summary about your approach to consulting, and a simple statement about your philosophy and how things are done at your practice, you will create an opportunity to check the client's expectations. You can further check your understanding of their expectations and project objectives in a written confirmation each time new objectives are discussed. Most importantly, if you have set your clients' expectations, you *must* have a system that can assure you of their fulfilment. Systems for effective consulting in organizations, which can be easily adapted to any practice, can be found in a number of useful texts, for example Block (1981).

Receiving payments
This section deals with face-to-face clients only. The process of receiving payments from clients is another step in the service 'journey' provided by your practice that lends itself to a systematic approach.

Any ambiguity and embarrassment involved in the financial transaction of payment for services rendered needs to be eliminated from the process. The first step towards this objective is to explain clearly the options at the initial contact or the first session, orally or through a handout. Subsequent to a session, a client needs to know whether the payment is now expected and, if so, how it should be made.

Some of the questions which may be in the client's mind at this point are:

- Must I pay now or can I pay later?
- Do I get a discount if I pay now?
- Can I pay by cheque?
- Can I pay by credit or debit card?
- Who will receive my payment?
- Will I get a receipt?
- Can I get a refund from any source, such as legal aid or private health insurance?

Your system of practice excellence will ensure that each client will be informed about the process of payment, and that each client's question will be answered courteously by a trained receptionist. The payment system will need to ensure that the receptionist is aware of the client's name, their compensation status and other payment-related data at the time of leaving the consulting room. This will reduce the client's waiting time, and will also aid the receptionist in dealing with a number of simultaneous demands: perhaps the client waiting to pay, new clients being served at the counter (who will presumably take longer to process), and a ringing telephone.

This last scenario may prove to be a useful and immediate test of the level of your practice's capability to deliver quality service with consistent predictability. What would your receptionist do if faced with such conflicting demands? Would he or she:

- Break off from a new client and ask that they wait while the paying client is served?
- Acknowledge the paying client but ask them to wait while continuing to serve the new client?
- Ignore the telephone and finish serving the new client?
- Answer the telephone and ask the caller to wait, then finish serving the new client?
- Politely break off from the new client, answer the telephone and then process the paying client before returning to the new client?

There are many possible permutations and many opportunities for the receptionist's own initiative and decisions in juggling priorities. Out of all the possibilities, there are only a few that will communicate the desired message about your practice. Since it is *your* practice, *you* need to design a system that will make sure your message gets out. The only sure way to do this is not to leave the receptionist's behaviour to chance.

One hears a universal criticism of staff who give primacy to telephone calls when someone is waiting for personal attention. This is doubly annoying when the telephone interrupts a face-to-face conversation and the staff member ranks the person present as secondary. In a situation where you play the role of a receptionist, after hours or when your receptionist is not available, the same applies to you. It is possible that you do not know the office systems and communicate the message: 'We practise in chaos'. If you perform the role of a receptionist, it is up to you to follow the procedures.

In an organizational psychology practice setting, the same principles apply – the difference being the lack of personal contact at the reception counter. Communication about your practice nevertheless happens when you issue invoices: their appearance; their content; the amount of detail about the service you have provided; the frequency of invoices being issued; the client's met expectation about the total amount; and the milestones achieved prior to billing. All of these add up to the client's approval of or disappointment with the payment process.

Making new appointments

Making new appointments for clients is another important activity in your practice–client interaction. The first aim of a systematic approach is to ensure that each client has no doubt about the date and time for which the appointment has been made. The second aim is to make sure that the practitioner has the time written in a diary, so that there is no possibility of the appointment being double-booked, or the practitioner not being available.

Your approach to making appointments should at least address the following questions:

- Is it a practitioner's or a receptionist's role to make appointments?
- Is it a combined role, with the practitioner establishing the general period until the next appointment, and with the receptionist actually identifying the specific time-slot and writing it in the appointment book?
- Whose role is it to write on the business card the date and time of the next appointment?
- Is the client informed about the cancellation rule, the consequences of not turning up without giving notice, and the acceptable length of time for cancelling before the appointment to avoid any penalties?
- Does a map identifying the practice address and any parking or public transport facilities nearby get forwarded to the first-time client?

- What are the rules about appointments after hours?
- Does the receptionist have a clear basis upon which to make appointments without referring to a practitioner?

There are probably some other questions that you and your staff would raise when you focus on this part of the practice system. Once they become known in the collective minds of those who determine the level of service delivered to your clients, they need to be systematically answered, documented, and then implemented.

4.13.4 The practice environment

The physical environment of your practice will very powerfully and immediately send a message about your practice, before the client even walks in. Its outside appearance, the signage, the lighting, the paint colour, the carpet and all the physical characteristics combined provide the client with information about your practice.

The reception area needs to engage the client immediately upon entry, with appropriately placed signs and a greeting. Any ambiguity about what is expected of the client upon entry should be meticulously eliminated. Directions to the waiting area, the reception, toilets, public telephones, etc. all need to be clearly marked. Further attention should be given to engaging the client in interesting activity while waiting. This can be done most easily with up-to-date magazines and/or reference books on special-interest topics placed on a low table. A television set may also be an effective way to ensure that your clients are engaged while waiting. A carefully selected and educational video can be played instead of the television programmes. Keep the sound down, though: otherwise, some clients may find it intrusive and offensive.

Special attention must be paid to public safety and cleanliness. A close observance of the practice's orderly and clean appearance is not costly, but it does require commitment. There is a need to identify clearly those responsible for the pleasant appearance of the waiting room, an orderly arrangement on the magazine table, and – particularly – children's toys. The cleaner's performance also needs to be monitored and fed back to encourage attention to detail.

Since your business deals with human factors of all kinds, it may be of interest to obtain some research on the effect of the physical environment on your client. This sort of research is, after all, in the psychology domain, and so part of your innovation process could be based on some well-documented scientific evidence.

4.13.5 Quality systems

To take your practice business system to another level, you may consider what would be involved in obtaining quality accreditation under the international ISO 9000 standards for your practice, although those processes are primarily designed for large organizations. Irrespective of whether or not you actually undertake the task, merely thinking about it may shape the way you do things in your practice. This sort of thinking is quality thinking. There are a number of quality-management books available that take a very practical approach to quality systems (for instance, Kruithof, 1993; Kruithof and Ryall, 1994).

4.13.6 Process charting and an operations manual

The process charting described earlier with reference to customer service should be applied to all other processes in the business. Other possible applications include: administration; marketing; training and development; people management; and performance review. The process chart will, in each case undertaken, form part of the foundation of the operations manual for your practice. Each activity in the chart will be described in specific behavioural terms, so that the person responsible for each activity will have a clear understanding of what your expectation is of their behaviour.

The operations manual will form the basis of induction and ongoing skills training for each staff member. Too many business operators rely on ad hoc verbal instructions, often communicated in a hurry in between appointments and other urgent tasks. Training of staff, particularly at the induction stage, is critical to the business function. It falls into the 'important but not urgent' category of tasks. Staff training is so much more effective when it is structured and built into elementary business systems. This is achieved by linking to the practice operations manual.

The operations manual can also define 'metrics' (i.e., quantifiable measures of performance) for each significant task. The measures are designed to indicate clearly the extent of compliance with the procedures and the level of work quality. These performance indicators must be easily obtainable, few in number, and as specific and concrete as possible. If they are designed with clarity and communicated explicitly, they can be used for regular staff performance reviews with great effectiveness. Used in this way, the operations manual can be a useful tool in shaping the behaviour of your staff. Its usefulness will become even clearer when you need to correct or improve their performance.

4.14 Client records

Client records must be kept, and must be kept secure. The special training that psychologists receive should ensure that they know what the content of such records should be. While the records are owned by the psychologist, they may be required to produce them for some purpose – such as a court case, or at the client's request. There is a valuable guide to electronic record keeping in Kat (1998).

Attention is drawn to the United Kingdom's Data Protection Act 1998. The address of the Data Protection Registrar for that Act is given in Appendix B. There are not many exemptions to that Act. In order to see whether or not the Act applies to what your practice does, readers should obtain a copy of *Notification Exemptions: A Self-Assessment Guide* from the Data Protection Registry.

4.15 The practice audit

Just as there is an annual financial audit, so too might you consider a complementary audit of the practice as a whole. There is an excellent model available in that used by the accounting profession. An accounting practice wanting such an audit obtains the services of a practice auditor. That auditor sets out the ground rules of what is to be audited (such as access to financial information, office procedures, compliance with employee legislation, etc.). The auditor is also alert to ethical issues, which include securing the permission of the accountant's clients before being given access to their files.

It is also the case that some quasi-governmental bodies require an audit. One can envisage a small practice run under the aegis of such an organization. In a one- to three person practice, it would be easy to lose sight of the proper procedures when caught up in day-to-day concerns. The external review is not only a check that proper procedures are being followed but also that the practice is being run efficiently. It is not to be seen as a criticism that such an audit is done; rather, it is a statement of professional commitment on everyone's part.

The advantages of such an audit are that it highlights areas of strength; areas where improvement might be effected; gives an independent view of ethical and legal compliance issues; and provides an overview of the practice that is often lost in day-to-day operations. At a more mundane level, such an audit (either by a 'clean bill of health' or suggestions for improved procedures) will provide a significant defence against potential or actual litigation. It will show to antagonistic parties that a genuine effort is continually being made to operate professionally. Although an audit involves an expense, it is one expense that pays large dividends in the longer term.

4.16 Skills development

4.16.1 Business management skills

It could be argued that the place where your success in business can really begin is when you reach the point of 'knowing that you don't know'. Then and only then are you likely to start searching for ways to run a practice better, and for any lack of business management skills.

Most people commence their business because they are technically good at something (at least according to their own perception, which hopefully accords with that of their clients). This drive and dedication are usually sufficient to get the business started. It is not until well down the track of the business development cycle that the practitioner becomes aware that to be able to manage a practice as a business requires a wholly different set of skills and competencies.

It is helpful at this point to identify the list of desirable skills, and then seek ways to complement your own repertoire. Sometimes, simply talking to your accountant can be a deliberate attempt to learn about the financial side of managing a business. Rather than seeing your accountant for as short a time as possible, therefore, you may see it as an opportunity to have someone answer your specific questions. As you are paying for the advice, you must really understand what you have set out to learn and not leave your accountant's office without having fulfilled your aims.

Another method is to attend various business seminars, which are so often advertised through direct mail or newsletters. In this connection, local enterprise schemes and the addresses given in Appendix B could be helpful. There are also organizations such as Business Link (see Appendix B) which give guidance on business development, marketing, financial management, legislation and the like. It is quite easy to find a seminar on marketing, or financial management, and the chances are you will learn something from each; but you will need to select seminars carefully so as to maximize the return for your investment. You might also subscribe to a number of magazines, or simply buy them from the newsagents' stands, which will broaden your business horizons and possibly provide another source of valuable seminars on relevant topics.

Many books and periodicals on the subject of business development are also available, in both the popular and the technical bookstores. There are a variety of magazine offerings, which include

'Opportunity 2000: Business, The Ultimate Journal'; 'The Franchise Magazine'; 'Real Money'; and 'All About Working From Home'. It will be seen that these have rather different coverage – and have relevance for the different aspects of small private business. Over and above that, there are many other sources of inspiration, which can be gleaned from otherwise uninspiring reading by someone used to assimilating complex scientific data and arguments. One advantage of popular business books is that they are usually very easy to read. For those who are too busy to read such books, there are book-summary services available on both cassette tapes and paper for a reasonable subscription fee.

The professional associations are also a useful source of information that combines both professional and practical skills and information. These include not only the British Psychological Society as a whole but also its divisions and sections for more specific advice. Furthermore, psychologists may belong to other relevant groups, such as management and personnel institutes. As a member of a professional association, it is up to you to define your benefit from it. Your gain will often be proportional to the level of your input. As the associations are normally voluntary organizations, they all rely on the goodwill of their members to perform most tasks. If you ever feel that 'they' are not supporting you or providing you with the required services, then it is time for you to become 'them', and become active.

Like most organizations, one would want a reason to join. Just as many practitioners choose to belong to the British Psychological Society, there are others who choose not to belong.

4.16.2 *Professional development*

At the same time that you are gaining skills in practice management, you will recognize that the development of your professional knowledge and skills is paramount to your ongoing capacity to practise. Your clients depend on your knowledge and skills, and also on these qualities in those you employ to provide professional services of excellent quality. 'Continuing professional development' (CPD) is now made obligatory by the British Psychological Society, and members must comply with both the Society's general policy and any relevant divisional policy.

The need for your own ongoing development cannot be overemphasized. Because of your time becoming such a rare commodity when in full-time practice, you will need to become more innovative about the way you gain the extra skills. You will choose conferences and seminars selectively to provide maximum benefit. You may also choose to invest in a modem and conduct specific literature searches via the Internet from your desktop computer, in order to optimize the time you spend reading and learning.

Probably the most creative way you can enhance your practice through such targeted research is to apply the psychological body of knowledge to your practice. Many psychologists work in the marketing, human-factor, personnel-selection and organizational fields. Their combined and published knowledge can add great value to the way you develop and manage your practice. The best ways to manage people, to motivate staff and to arrange the office are all examples of useful information. To find them and to apply them will be your challenge in your quest to achieve excellence in your practice.

4.16.3 Personal development

It is surprising and incongruous that professionals providing services in the area of people development often neglect their own. Managing your practice and simultaneously working within the practice will not leave you with much spare time. You will be in charge of the vast number of activities that you will be planning, developing, and executing, all at the same time. The excitement and the load that a private practice brings can easily derail your personal life. It is more important than ever to spend some time on your personal renewal.

Covey (1993), in his business management best-seller, referred to this as the seventh habit of highly effective people: 'take time to sharpen your saw'. It is a very important but not urgent activity. Its aim is to preserve and enhance your greatest asset – yourself. Take time to ensure that the physical, social, emotional, mental and spiritual dimensions of your life are all balanced, so that you can practise for many more years to come.

Some of the activities to check for are: exercise, breaks, holidays, nutrition, and stress management; family time, friends, social support; personal security, self-esteem, excitement, laughing; reading for pleasure, visualizing, writing, painting; commitment, reflection, service, study, and meditation. If you are skilled at denying that work has taken over your life, while everybody else around you tells you it has, it is easy to do a quick check by adding up the hours spent at the end of each day under the above categories (though other categories may be more applicable to you). If you find that the percentages are stacked in the work category, it is time to stop and sharpen your saw. It will be much easier and faster to use it later.

4.17 Networking

Networking with other practitioners provides vital contact to alleviate the sense of isolation. It will also help in validating and normalizing your experiences. You can create formal networks around the area where you practise, to provide easier opportunities to meet. Such networks usually provide further opportunities for informal contact as your needs arise.

Attendance at formal meetings, seminars and conferences can provide the dual benefit of gaining new skills and new network contacts. Someone has generated the following Ten Commandments for networking:

- Thou shalt exchange business cards.
- Thou shalt not stand in a corner.
- Thou shalt seek out and find others.
- Thou shalt make friends when they are not needed.
- Thou shalt take an interest in others.
- Thou shalt always follow up.
- Thou shalt keep in touch.
- Thou shalt act like a host, not a guest.
- Thou shalt edit thy contacts.
- Thou shalt share thy contacts.

Your encounters in various professional gatherings will increase in value if you apply these rules. Most professionals tend to network with like-minded, predictable and similar individuals, and such people provide worthwhile support. You may nonetheless find it invigorating to seek out quite a different network of individuals, who will usually come from a different professional background from yourself. They may include lawyers, salespeople, professional speakers, or other business people. Such networks are likely to energize your thinking, challenge your vision, and therefore fulfil a different but most valuable role.

4.18 Maintaining ethical standards

One means of demonstrating your practice's commitment to excellence is through its maintenance of ethical standards in all its dealings. This can take two forms, described further in the rest of this section:

- publishing formal statements of intent;
- setting out a charter of clients' rights and responsibilities.

It would be hard to overemphasize the importance of ethics to successful practice. Quite apart from the moral imperatives that drive us, there is the basic commercial consideration that a good reputation is good for business. The goodwill deriving from such a reputation is a marketable commodity, and good ethics is excellent risk management.

One of the major difficulties that practitioners experience is that ethics is potentially so complicated that it is put on the back burner of the commercial stove. The clearly set-out *Code of Conduct, Ethical Principles and Guidelines* of the British Psychological Society is valuable here. The complementary work, *Ethics for Psychologists* (Francis, 1999), and the various guides produced by divisions of the British Psychological Society should all help ameliorate that difficulty.

If a problem should arise, the British Psychological Society has produced *Guidance on the Complaints, Investigatory and Disciplinary Procedures* (1999). That document, quite rightly, sets out the formal processes of complaint receipt and investigation. To that we might add a voice pointing out the merit of informal and constructive solutions that might be used before institution of formal proceedings. None of this is to denigrate proper procedures, but rather to point out a better way of handling difficulties leading to solutions acceptable to all of the parties and maintaining the reputation of the profession.

4.18.1 Formal statements of intent

Among the statements you might wish to consider are those that indicate to your clients that you are intent on operating according to good and explicit standards. Such statements might include:

- *Mission statement* of the practice: to include the purpose of the practice (e.g., to provide high-quality reports to lawyers or to provide professional support for victims of sexual abuse). It could also specify the mode of delivery (e.g., on an individual basis or the use of group techniques).
- *Statement of the code of practice* to which the practitioners are bound (e.g., the British Psychological Society Code of Professional Conduct, and/or other codes, such as that set out by the British Institute of Management).
- *Statement on business ethics* (as opposed to professional ethics).
- *Statement of privacy*: that privacy will be maintained except under certain specified conditions (e.g., under a legal compulsion to reveal) – and making reference to the current national Data Protection Act.
- *Statement on legal compliance*: your adherence to various aspects of legal compliance (such as equal-opportunities employment).
- *Statement on fees*: how they will be calculated, when they fall due, and other related matters (as outlined in the fees section of this handbook).

None of this will matter one iota if the commitment to the contents of the statements is not genuine, for the consuming public has strong inbuilt sincerity-detectors. While statements such as we have suggested are useful, their existence must be matched by good-spirited and well-intentioned implementation. For example, no matter how good a statement on fees is, it is how a complicated situation is handled that will determine a client's view of your operation.

4.18.2 Charter of clients' rights and responsibilities

From the view of human dignity as well as that of commercial prudence, it is advisable to have a published charter of clients' rights and responsibilities. Such a statement would be prominently displayed in an appropriate place – perhaps a copy of the charter might be held at reception, and available in summary form for handing to clients and potential clients when requested.

Those who would like a starting point are recommended to Francis (1999). For those in health-related fields, the National Health Service document entitled *The Patient's Charter and You* (1999) is relevant. For those in clinical practice, attention is drawn to the document by the Division of Clinical Psychology of the British Psychological Society called *Responsibility and Accountability in Clinical Psychology*. This document is available in draft form as it is currently being updated; see also the Division of Clinical Psychology's booklet entitled *Professional Practice Guidelines* (1995).

Among the points that such a charter should make are those of client responsibilities as well as rights. It will address issues that need clarification, such as the liability for fees for missed appointments. Even so, listening and negotiating are preferable to pointing to inflexible 'rules'. People from the most diverse backgrounds object to the same issues: firmly located here are the twin complaints of 'no one ever told me' and 'no one ever asked me'. While you have professional and ethical principles that you will maintain, so too do we recommend that explaining, seeking common ground, and listening sympathetically are part of the process of implementing your standards.

5

Expanding your practice

Once your practice has passed through the stage of 'getting organized', and has developed business systems that ensure that you can deliver services with consistent quality, you might progress to the stage of 'maturity'. In this phase, the business systems work well yet are constantly refined, the clients are satisfied, and you are not overworked. It might seem somewhat utopian but it is true for many organizations.

If you find it hard to believe that it is possible not to be overworked and still run a successful practice, this chapter has been written to show you how. The paradox of being successful in private practice – or any business, for that matter – is that the better you are, the more in demand you are. The greater the demand, the worse you become, and your personal life could suffer so much that you will wonder whether business success is really worth it.

You may react to this demand differently and begin to think of expansion. You have so much work, so why not share it with others. You could identify the areas where you need help, such as administration or practice management, counselling, training or consulting, and try to find someone with any of these capabilities. To put this another way, you could delegate those functions that others with appropriate skills can readily perform.

It is even more manageable if you have already developed the business and quality systems discussed in Chapter 4. Any additional person would find it relatively easy to apply the system as laid out in the operations manual. Induction training would also be so much easier if the new staff member in your practice could read the manual rather than learning procedures personally from you.

Quite often at this stage of practice development there is a real fear about employing someone, and being responsible for getting work for someone else. If this type of thinking is crippling your decision making, there are other ways of expanding your practice than by employing people. These will be explored later in this chapter. Such a fear needs to be overcome if you are ever going to be freed from the tyranny of simultaneously *being* the practice and *running* the practice.

If someone else comes into the practice, you will have to share this identity. When you market your practice, it will no longer be just you being promoted. What you will promote is a business that provides a professional service, and it may be actually provided by someone else – your colleagues or staff.

5.1 Staffing

There are many facets to employing others. The more important aspects to staffing are set out in the rest of this section.

5.1.1 Recognizing the need

The decision to employ administrative staff rather than professional staff is usually made early in the development phase. Initially, you might take on all roles in the practice by yourself. Because your time is not translated into money and you have little of it to invest, it is easier to wear many hats yourself. You might say: 'It does not cost me anything'. This could well be a reasonable approach initially, but you must become aware of the moment when the lost opportunity of your time's real financial worth prevents the business from growing and freeing you up, through its growth, to achieve your life goals.

Some highly successful practices have identified the moment when they employed the first person they could not afford as the turning point in their financial performance and their best business decision. The reason for this turnaround was that they were forced to do more marketing and spend more time in the professional role, thus earning much more for the practice. Then the true value of their previously lost earnings opportunity became obvious. The more time you spend on bookkeeping, typing and writing invoices, the less time you have to earn income.

The recognition that you need assistance with professional work usually comes rather later in the business-development cycle. It may occur perhaps for the first time when you are about to plan your next holiday, only to realize that your business gets in the way. If you go away for a number of weeks, who will oversee your practice and see clients when needed? The compromise may be to take a few short breaks, so that your clients never really miss you. While away you check your phone messages, or receive them regularly through your pager system. You may feel the need to respond to them, so you get on the mobile phone ... and you are back at work. While this may work for a while, you will probably realise, deep within, that it cannot last for too long. Your independent practice suddenly shows few signs of flexibility and independence – your main aims for starting it in the first place. It has become too dependent on you, and you have become imprisoned by it.

The need for professional assistance may also be experienced sporadically: when the work increases for a period of time, or when you are involved in a specific short-term project. It may last for only a few weeks, but it becomes quite obvious during that time that you cannot carry out all the tasks yourself. Some projects may involve assessments of a large number of employees, and the time frames are impossible to meet for one practitioner.

This is another point of business decision making. You can either contract the work out to someone else, form a temporary alliance with another practice, or employ someone on a full-time, part-time or casual basis. If you choose the latter option, or if you have already recognized the need for administrative, reception and bookkeeping assistance, you will have no option but to accept your new identity in life – you will now be an employer.

5.1.2 Fundamentals of the employer–employee relationship

There are well-established characteristics defining the relationship between employers and employees, the fundamental one being that the employer pays the employee for work performed.

This important transaction gives rise to many expectations on both sides. The employee's livelihood becomes dependent on the employer, and there is an expectation of needing to be looked after. The employer parts with hard-earned money and has an expectation that the employee will behave according to instructions. This relationship is particularly evident in small organizations, where the exertion of its few members generates the majority of its income.

All too often, some of these expectations are not entirely met to everyone's satisfaction. The employee may ask for more money, more leave entitlements, or special treatment for compassionate reasons. The employer may demand that the tasks be performed in a different or better way. While this chapter is not meant to be a treatise on employee relations and human resource management, there has to be a clear recognition on the part of practice owners that they are subject to all the rules and regulations governing an employer–employee relationship. Having become an employer, you must behave like one.

One of the first tasks will be to register your practice as a group employer with the Inland Revenue. You will also need to ensure that you conform to the employment conditions as set out by the relevant government departments – of employment and education, and of trade and industry. Also significant here is the necessity to be alert to trade-union matters.

Becoming an employer carries with it numerous responsibilities that must be taken seriously. Even so, the fear of responsibilities being too onerous should not prevent you from becoming an employer, because the potential benefits far outweigh the problems associated with this new identity.

5.1.3 Staff remuneration

One of the most obvious functions that an employer must perform is to ensure that every employee is adequately rewarded for effort. Many wages and salaries are governed by legal agreements that you may obtain from the appropriate government department. You may wish to obtain a copy of the entire award, from the relevant department, an employers' association, your local chamber of commerce, or a trade union.

Apart from agreeing on the hourly rate (where necessary bearing in mind the National Minimum Wage regulations in force in the United Kingdom since April 1999 and periodically updated), you need to agree on the frequency and the basis on which remuneration will be paid – weekly or fortnightly, by cheque or direct credit into the bank – and on which day of the week or day in the month pay will be distributed.

Irrespective of whether pay is delivered by cheque or through a direct bank transaction, you will need to provide all employees with their pay advice slip, showing clearly how their amount of pay was calculated. Again, irrespective of the number of people on your staff you will need to manage the overall payroll function, which means keeping the records of paid amounts, taxation details, all entitlements, and pension scheme contributions. The most cost-efficient method for small numbers of staff is to keep a manual record of every payment. There are specially prepared forms for this purpose that you can purchase from office stationery suppliers and some newsagents, and the Inland Revenue supplies its record forms (P11s, etc.) free of charge.

There are a number of different bases for rewarding people for their work. Four in particular are set out here, as follows:

- **Regular salary.** This is calculated on an hourly basis either for full-time or part-time (with a set number of hours each week) effort, or for casual (a variable number of hours each week) work. The casual rates should have built-in compensation for public holidays and leave entitlements, and so these hourly rates tend to be higher. The higher cost of wages is balanced by having no cost associated with sick pay and annual leave.

- *Regular salary plus performance-based bonus*. This would necessitate a very clearly defined system for determining the amount and timing of bonuses. For example: for support staff the bonus arrangement could be an amount calculated on an annual basis, and would depend on the level of their performance as measured by some predefined indicators; for professional staff the bonus could be a regular extra payment in each pay period, calculated on the basis of the time charged out to clients.

- *Commission-based contract*. These hourly rates must be much higher than the regular hourly rates (at least twice, if not three times, the normal wage rate). This basis of payment is only applicable to professional staff who are able to generate income through their work, and it involves payment for the time actually charged out by the practice. In consequence, there is the need for a higher pay rate to compensate the person for all the other work that is *not* directly chargeable, such as writing reports, administration and marketing. Note, however, that this type of employment should not be confused with a co-practice partnership arrangement that is discussed below. If the person is employed on a contract basis, that person is primarily your employee (see below), not another psychologist in private practice.

- *A combination of the above methods*. In this case, either a regular salary rate or a contract rate applies, plus an additional annual bonus system that is defined on the basis of the overall practice's financial performance.

5.1.4 Employee entitlements

Employee entitlements are likely to include leave of absence – sick leave, annual leave, long-service leave, family or compassionate leave, maternity leave, paternity leave, and special leave. While these are not actually paid for each week, your accounting procedures may need to reflect the liability that your practice is accruing during the period of employment. This may not be necessary if the amounts are small, as your accountant may advise. When they are substantial or when you need to show an accurate balance sheet, you will need to present all kinds of liability that you have accrued. These include staff-related overheads that will have to be paid even if the person is not at work.

A point of caution here is the way in which entitlements might build up. For example, you do not want to suddenly find yourself liable to send a valued employee on three months' long-service leave on full pay. You deprive yourself of a key staff member and need to find the money to pay them – and their replacement.

To illustrate the need for staff policies, you may need to determine whether an employee should be paid a leave entitlement before fully accruing it. After what period of employment will your staff be able to claim their entitlement for sick leave or annual leave? Is sick leave cumulative? How long is long service? Can sick leave be used when a family member needs care?

The answers to these questions are not difficult, but they require attention to detail. It may well be most efficient to write down as many rules as you can think of, from the days when you were in the employee's position and when others in personnel and human resource departments were making such rules for you. Then deal with each exception to the rules as it comes up, and keep adding to your staff policy as you become aware of its limitations.

5.1.5 Taxation

Probably the three most serious responsibilities of an employer are to pay PAYE (pay as you earn) tax on behalf of the employee, and to ensure National Insurance payments are made. Managers must also ensure that all due VAT is paid.

The employer has an obligation to deduct the correct amount of tax from each amount of gross pay, put aside this amount in their account, and pay the group tax on a monthly or quarterly basis, carefully following the instructions laid out in the group employer's information kit provided by the Inland Revenue. Late payments of any tax liabilities are heavily and immediately penalized. Correct information needs to be obtained from the employee at the commencement of employment with regard to the appropriate tax file numbers and other special additional tax obligations. Furthermore, an employer must keep the taxation and payment records of each employee for a statutory period of years from when the record originated or from the time of the employment being terminated.

The obligation to take group tax out of the gross pay also applies to those engaged on a contract basis, unless there is no employer–employee relationship between the contractor and your psychology practice. There has been much confusion and ambiguity in this area, and it is likely to continue. There are some well-known 'litmus tests' of this relationship, which you can apply to your situation to determine whether or not you need to take tax out of someone's pay. If the contractor is essentially under your control, as an employee would be, and if this contractor works exclusively in your practice, there is little doubt that they too are your employees.

Another way to determine the relationship is whether you pay the contractor regularly on the basis of time spent in your practice or on presentation of an invoice. In other words, is the contractor really in business by themselves and can they demonstrate this, maintaining their own equipment and such like? Payments on an invoice are mostly irregular and short term – for example, a contracted computer expert who comes in for a few hours as need arises. This is an important issue to clarify in the development of your staff policy, because there is a tendency for the contractor-employee to prefer to pay their own tax, and the corresponding preference for the employer not to pay the group tax in order to avoid the extra administrative burden. Since these personal preferences tend in the same direction, it is easy to reach consensus when the employer and the prospective contractor negotiate their employment conditions. Such consensus is not always right in law, however, and you as employer have greater penalties to fear and more to lose if you do not comply with the employers' taxation regulations. It is recommended that you always seek advice from your accountant, an employers' association, or a relevant government body (including the Inland Revenue) when in doubt – and preferably get a response in writing

While on the topic of taxation regulations, we must mention that it is a good practice to behave in all your financial decisions and record keeping as though you were expecting a taxation audit very soon. It is impossible to predict if and when such an audit will occur and it is better to be prepared than surprised. One way to prepare for such an eventuality is to ask your external accountant to conduct a 'pre-audit' once every few years. This might also provide an opportunity to improve your business systems, and lead to greater efficiencies in your practice administration.

Finally, it also makes sense to make provision for your own tax liabilities. There may be tax to be paid in the expectation of the tax for which you will be liable, if you earn any income that has not already been taxed throughout the year. This is known as 'Schedule D' tax liability, and it applies to the self-employed. If you are an employer, one way to minimize the impact of paying tax in lump sums is to pay yourself a salary as an employee (and therefore have tax deducted as well), on a regular basis throughout the year. Ask your accountant for advice on this procedure.

5.1.6 Pension scheme arrangements

There is a current move to require employees to subscribe to some kind of private pension scheme. The employer's responsibilities may come to include a compulsory payment to a pension fund nominated by the employee. Some companies require employees to join their company pension scheme. The time may come when there is an obligation to run an employer's scheme for pensions. Seek your accountant's advice. Unless an employee begins his or her working career at your practice, the employee is likely to have an existing fund from at least one previous place of employment; this payment will be a fixed proportion of salary.

Among the issues that it is vital to monitor in any such arrangement is that of not only ensuring that the sums are properly deducted, if that is required, but also being attentive to whether or not the employer must also make a contribution to the same fund.

5.1.7 *Insurance cover*

As the practice grows, so might the need to reconsider the insurances mentioned earlier in Chapter 4. In the case of employing professional staff, you will need to cover their insurance for malpractice liability, professional indemnity, legal expenses, and public liability. As previously mentioned, the relevant professional associations (e.g., the British Psychological Society) have very favourable arrangements with insurance underwriters so as to provide policies and premiums for individual members. Such policies become quite expensive when you are an employer and have to cover a number of individuals in your practice. You may find it more cost-effective to obtain a group liability cover through an insurance broker.

The British Psychological Society has a document (no date) entitled *Professional Liability Insurance for Psychologists*, and there is a BPS form that nominates the Smithson Mason Group in relation to such insurance. That form has answers to frequently asked questions. Competitive quotes are always appropriate, but one needs to be mindful of the conditions that apply as well as to the premium paid.

It may be one of the conditions of employment that your employees are responsible for their own professional indemnity insurance cover. You need to be mindful that some organizations seeking your services will require proof of your professional indemnity and public liability insurance, and they may further nominate a certain level. It may be unreasonable to demand that each individual employee carry such levels of cover to fulfil the contractual obligations to which your practice, rather than those individuals, is a party. Furthermore, if your employees are covered personally for professional indemnity and public insurance, you will still need to assure yourself that their policies are current in order to ensure that you are not in breach of contract.

As a group employer, you have an obligation to cover your staff for appropriate compensation insurance under an employers' liability policy. The amount of the premium will, in part, be calculated on the basis of your practice's total remuneration amount, and the relevant industry grouping. A further issue is that of employer obligations with respect to rehabilitation and return-to-work programmes if a worker is injured. It is recommended that you familiarize yourself with such regulations.

5.1.8 Seeking assistance about employer's obligations

The above brief discussion of employment issues is only a very general and partial introduction to the long evolution of industrial relations law and practice in the United Kingdom. There are many other decisions you will be called to make as an employer, which are subject to a plethora of legislation covering employee issues. A wrong decision can be very costly. On the other hand, a decision to employ the right person can be most rewarding to your business.

Other issues, although occurring less often but nevertheless having serious potential impact are as follows: termination of employment; contracts of employment; enterprise bargaining; union representation; dishonesty; procedural and substantive fairness of dismissal; equal opportunities; sexual harassment; occupational health and safety; and workplace contracts – to name just a few. It is best to seek professional advice when in doubt about how to handle any of these issues, and to make yourself aware of the current legislation and employer obligations at all times. The useful sources of such advice are employer associations (such as your local chamber of commerce), your accountant or your solicitor, and in addition the Inland Revenue offices can be very helpful.

There is also a range of customized support, comprising business links between local authorities, so-called Enterprise Agencies, chambers of commerce, etc. Enterprise Agencies not only provide free or low-cost expert advice but some also mount seminars, presentations of business plans for scrutiny, and even have a prize for the best business plan made at a presentation. There is also a scheme called 'Prime', an initiative for those aged 50+. It has the slogan 'The prime time to be self-employed' and carries the subtitle of 'An initiative for mature enterprise'. The Prince of Wales is the President (see Appendix B). A central number to call for business advice is 0345-567-765, which will provide information about your local agency. If you would like to look at a website of business advisers, again see Appendix B (under IBA).

In general, four principles are recommended for sound employment practice:

- *Be informed* – constantly update your knowledge, and take it seriously.
- *Be fair* – act in a way that recognizes reciprocal rights and obligations.
- *Plan* – document your employment policies, and inform all employees.
- *Keep good records* – not only the employment, practice and financial records, but also the basis for decisions.

5.1.9 Employing support staff

As stated earlier in this section on staffing, employing support staff is usually a simple decision that most full-time practices embrace at an early point in their development. The most common experience consists of employment of one person who shares the tasks in the following areas:

- reception work (e.g., telephone answering, making appointments, and client reception);
- office administration (filing, etc.);
- typing or word processing;
- client data maintenance (either manual or computer-based);
- invoicing clients;
- following up unpaid debts.

Bookkeeping and paying accounts can also be included in the same person's role, provided that it does not place unreasonable demands on that person's time and skills. This scenario usually involves compilation of the documents that are forwarded to the external accountant. The accountant usually provides a quarterly or, maybe, a yearly financial statement.

Another and perhaps more cost-effective approach in a larger practice is to employ a dedicated person, most likely on a part-time basis, to manage the accounting function in-house. Apart from managing all accounts payable, the in-house bookkeeper can also be put in charge of the payroll function (with adequate procedural safeguards over disbursements), which will lessen the burden on the practice owners involved with personnel and administrative issues.

5.1.10 Employing professionals

Employing a professional to perform some of the services that you probably perform yourself carries with it more risk, and it is usually shunned by practitioners. Such a professional needs to represent you and your practice. In many respects your practice will depend on their competence, commitment and integrity – as it has on yours. While the risk is there, you need simply to be more careful when selecting such a person.

It is certainly possible to locate highly competent and trustworthy individuals who prefer to be employed rather than running practices. They might just be the ones who, having read the second chapter of this book, have decided that their enterprising interest and skill are not adequate to embark on this journey. There is no universal truth in the popular belief that if you are really good then you will be working for yourself.

If you wish to embark on employing professionals within your practice, you would be prudent to take the task of recruiting and selecting extremely seriously, and to proceed with caution. When you have found the right person, you might just discover that you do not need to turn into a salesperson to constantly find jobs or clients for your new employee. They will probably be acutely aware of their need to charge far more than they earn to ensure their job viability. If you are not prepared to take such a step, and you have a need for professional assistance in your practice because of the volume of work, there are other options that are explored below.

5.1.11 Co-practice arrangements

Some practitioners feel most comfortable with the scenario where any new co-professional shares maximum responsibility for marketing and finding new clients. Your dilemma is that your practice has already earned its reputation and developed its image. To the extent that it already has a defined product and a market, the invited new professional should find it easier to market their services than you did originally. This, in a sense, is the value of goodwill.

Common mistakes that are often made at this point consist of either giving away too much or overestimating the goodwill. If you are in the former category, you will essentially enter into a belated partnership arrangement where everything is shared equally. If you fall into the latter error, you will underpay the prospective co-practitioner and expect them to be a partner. Our experience tends to suggest that there are more cases in the latter category.

You must not forget that, in this expansion scenario, you are not entering into an employer–employee relationship and so it is inappropriate to set a salary rate. The co-practitioner should be left to set his or her own fees, and your practice should instead charge for the services that it provides to the new practitioner. The first component of such a fee is the administration and reception support. If your practice has such facilities and the new professional makes full use of them, the situation is parallel to that of a serviced office. The value of such services can therefore be easily benchmarked against commercially available facilities. Essentially a rent fee can be set, depending on the level of support provided.

The second and most contentious component is related to marketing. If your co-practitioner gains clients through his or her own marketing effort, the newcomer is entitled to a reasonably large percentage of the charged fee, for there is a need to be compensated for the time spent on marketing activities, as you would have expected in your practice. If, on the other hand, the new professional simply works with the existing clients of your practice, the relationship with you becomes more like that of an employee and employer. There may be a reasonable argument in such cases for a marketing levy applied to your co-practitioner for every chargeable hour, in addition to the rent and support fee.

This is a rather complicated scenario but is nevertheless frequently entered into by many practitioners desperate to gain assistance with their work but not willing to become an employer. If such an option is being considered, it is recommended instead to apply a partnership model more formally, by entering into a properly constructed contract. There are good examples of such models operating successfully, notably in the legal profession. It is best to call such relationships what they really are – partnerships – and structure them accordingly. Yet be alert to being responsible for all partnership debts if your partner avoids them.

5.1.12 Contractor and locum arrangement

Another common scenario is where the practitioner enters into a temporary arrangement with another psychologist, who becomes a locum or a short-term contractor. The precipitating events are usually a large temporary workload, a holiday, or some other prolonged absence of the practice owner.

It is the best response to the short-term need, so that your practice can truly meet your life goals, which almost certainly should not include being tied to consulting rooms at all times. This scenario is very much like a short-term employment contract and needs to be developed as such. Because the contractor will not enjoy the usual job tenure and employee entitlements, they should be remunerated by a much greater hourly rate than a full-time employee. As a starting point for negotiations, we suggest 50 per cent of the charged fee. For this they would bear considerable responsibility – both professional and reputational. If this works well, both parties will have gained. If it does not work well, some business will be lost to the owner – and reputational damage will be done to the temporary incumbent and possibly the owner.

If the locum's remuneration is totally commission-based – that is, they are paid just for the hours you can charge – their fee will depend on the amount of time you expect them to spend on non-chargeable activities. If they simply turn up to see your clients and charge for almost every hour they spend at work, this fee could justifiably be quite low (say, double the salary rate, to compensate them for loss of normal entitlements). If, on the other hand, you expect them to run your practice for you, and perform a large number of non-chargeable activities, their remuneration should rise accordingly (say, up to three or four times their salary rate).

As with the co-practice arrangement, the principle of fairness must apply between employer and employees, partners, principals, and colleagues – just as it does in all other walks of life. So when dealing with partners or co-practitioners, equity should be maintained. There are some fundamental rules that prevent inequity: among these are the firm commitment to equal contributions and equal risks. To ensure this occurs, there are some practical questions that one might ask:

- Who carries the financial risk?
- Who puts in the professional time?
- Whose reputation is at risk?
- How is marketing time to be costed as a contribution?
- What is the value of a client base, and how is its contribution to be estimated?

The person who is exposed to more risk should also expect better rewards. The potential disappointments from such short-term relationships can be easily prevented by setting expectations before the relationship starts. All tasks should be documented as in the job description for the employee. Below are some of the questions that should be addressed and documented by both contractors and employing practitioners before entering into a contract:

- When does a contractor get paid?
- On what basis is the payment calculated: per chargeable session, per any session, per hour, or per week?
- What are the exact monetary rates involved?
- What is expected regarding note keeping and writing reports?
- What is expected regarding accounting records (e.g., telephone calls, number of sessions and activities)?
- Who is responsible for professional indemnity insurance?
- Who is responsible for public (or employers') liability compensation insurance?
- Is the contractor entitled to any paid leave (sick leave, annual leave, etc.)?
- Who is responsible for the marketing of the practice's services?
- What arrangements apply if the contractor develops a clearly defined clientele for the practice?
- What is expected to occur at the termination of the contract, particularly in relation to clients who choose to continue with the contractor, to new clients/contracts gained as a direct result of the contract employment, and to records and other intellectual property?
- What is the duration of the contract?
- What undertakings are needed to prevent poaching of clients?

- Is there an embargo on the temporary incumbent practising in the same field of psychology, or within a nominated geographical location, or within a fixed period of time?

5.1.13 Job descriptions

Whatever the employment contract and whatever the job involved – whether support or professional – there are some basic principles to follow to increase the productivity of employees and their usefulness to the practice. The first of these is planning a job before a person is recruited and selected. You must first identify what the job consists of and what sort of person would best fit the tasks. Such planning requires that you document all the tasks in a Job Description, or Duty Statement.

Such a document will include at least:

- job name;
- tasks;
- level of accountability;
- supervisory arrangements;
- measures of satisfactory job performance;
- pre-requisite qualifications;
- minimum knowledge, skills and attitude.

The last two items are of particular use during the selection process. They will form the selection criteria.

5.1.14 Selection and placement

It is probably true that you only realize how vital the task of recruiting and selecting the right person is when you have experienced placing the *wrong* person. The amount of unproductive time and the potential damage to a business suffered by such an error is of such proportions that virtually any amount of investment in a thorough selection process will never be too much.

A well-constructed job description (see previous subsection) will be the basis for developing useful selection criteria that will, in turn, be related to the required tasks. You may consider using one or more psychometric tests as well. A well-used selection interview technique is likely to be employed. Job selection can be drastically improved if you plan to structure it in such a way that each key selection criterion is well represented in your questions. A structured interview uses behaviourally based questions as much as possible, and the same questions should be applied to every applicant. Ideally, you should interview in a panel so that more opinions can be gathered. The candidates' performance is tested systematically against each criterion.

By following the selection process as systematically as you feel you can, rather than relying totally on your intuition and interviewing skills, you are likely to improve the probability of recruiting a suitable person to the job. We are well aware of the poor validity of interviewing as a positive selection technique, but we do subscribe to the view that it is a much better system for rejecting an inappropriate applicant. In your personnel selection system, which you will have developed in your practice to reach for excellence, you will want to ensure that all references or referees are followed up without fail. A second interview may also be appropriate.

Once you have made an offer of employment to a candidate, it is sound practice to confirm it by sending a letter, which should include at least the following:

- confirmation of the job being offered, with any remaining conditions (e.g. subject to a satisfactory medical report and references) being spelled out;
- date and time of expected commencement;
- the place of employment;
- the duration of trial period;
- the remuneration details, including review systems;
- the supervisory structure in place;
- the summary of major areas of involvement.

You should not forget that some of the other applicants who missed out on a job might be your future clients, or colleagues, or future employees. Even if they were never to become connected to you again, the image of your practice needs to be consistently communicated to everyone around you. Whether and what you write to the unsuccessful applicants, and how long you take to write to them, will also send them a message about your practice and your professionalism. This will happen whether you intended it or not.

5.1.15 Induction training

Once the selection has been made and the candidate has accepted the job, and your new employee is about to commence employment, the matter of training must be addressed. Whatever other training the person will undertake, the initial induction training will determine, to a large extent, compliance with your practice systems. Rather than relying on informal chat, as the person turns up on the first day, it is far more effective to have the induction process structured. Your operational manual will now turn into a most useful document that can provide a structure to your induction training.

An induction session is an excellent opportunity to reinforce to a new employee (for something will already have been communicated during the selection process) the values held within your practice and the philosophy underpinning your approach to business. It is also the ideal time to introduce your practice's vision and mission statements, as well as its ethics statement that governs the behaviour of all involved in your practice. The practice manual should not be long or complex in its approach. It should provide a new employee with a clear knowledge of your expectations. It will inform the new recruit of how personal performance is measured and reviewed.

5.1.16 Performance review

The process of performance and development reviews is a familiar concept to all who have worked in large organizations. To many, the memory of it is often stained with bureaucratic procedures and little effective change. This is unfortunate because psychologists know well how feedback, when used appropriately, can become a powerful tool in gaining new skills and shaping someone's behaviour. While the concept of regular performance reviews is potentially the best strategy towards increasing an employee's effectiveness, its application has led many organizations to ineffectual results.

The other psychological concept that performance-review designers have heavily relied on is goal setting. Any review process revolves around setting realistic, measurable goals for your employees' behaviour, developed with their full participation, and then giving regular and frequent feedback with regard to the achievement of those goals.

Some of the outcomes from the reviews may have to do with the skills development of the employees, which has been identified as the reason for the gap between the expected and actual performance. If you have agreed for an employee to attend a relevant training course, for example, you need to follow it through and pay for it, when the time comes. Your failure to do so can seriously undermine the value of the whole process.

You can also use the review process to gain insight into your management style by requesting that your employees provide you with an honest appraisal of your *own* performance in relation to staff management. If you are able to suppress your ego's defensive mechanisms at such reviews, these sessions can be useful opportunities to improve yourself and your practice.

Your formal system of performance reviews does not mean that you disregard the everyday feedback and ongoing informal interaction with your employee. You can at the same time be a 'one minute manager' who helps people reach their full potential by 'catching them doing something right'. The immediacy of feedback should also form part of your management repertoire (Blanchard and Johnson, 1982).

5.2 Marketing

Now that, in our ongoing scenario, you have expanded the practice by employing more staff, the issue of marketing will probably return to the fore in your thinking – that is, if it ever went away. Marketing is something that happens on an ongoing basis. You might dream ideas and do some networking at a social barbecue when you least expect it. You will always have your business cards with you, just in case someone asks you about what you do and sounds interested. You will nevertheless need to exercise caution when involving your social networks in the marketing of your practice, for two main reasons: first, you need to be careful not to alienate your friends and their contacts; and, second, you may face ethical dilemmas when providing services to those to whom you are socially related. Even keeping these two restrictions in mind, there are still plenty of opportunities to find potential business leads in everyday interactions with people.

Ideally, the marketing strategy that will form part of your business plan will now be in place and in its implementation phase. Your initial marketing will have also taken place to inform the world around of the arrival of your practice on the market. But now you need more ideas to give your practice an extra boost so that you can guarantee some stability of income, not just for yourself but also for the people you now employ or contract.

In your approach to marketing, you need to be aware of the long-term nature of its coming to fruition. Quite often, and particularly in the corporate market, ideas that you have communicated through your brochure, letters, website or speaking engagements may not produce any outcomes for a number of months or years. Some, of course, will *never* lead to positive outcomes. You should not expect immediate results, particularly when the marketing activity aims at creating a higher profile. Instead, it is helpful to think that your marketing efforts of today will have their effect in one year's time. This simple recognition will lead you to market actively at times when you are very busy, even though it seems counterintuitive, so that you can continue to be busy in the future.

The remainder of this section provides you with some practical ideas that you can use in any future revised marketing strategy.

5.2.1 *Speaking engagements*

One of the easiest ways to become known in the local, corporate or professional community is through offering your public-speaking services. Depending on the situation, you can either charge for it or deliver it free. For example, a local school or a health community centre may need someone to conduct a parenting-skills seminar, or a session on learning skills for the students. A local dietician or a medical practice may be interested in conducting public sessions on eating disorders. The opportunities are limited only by your imagination. To expand it a little, start by asking about the need for public seminars in your area.

In the corporate market, there are numerous conferences and training seminars whose organizers search for credible, knowledgeable, and obviously high-quality speakers on all sorts of management and people-related subjects, from occupational stress to family-friendly policies. Such conference papers are expected to be delivered free of charge, although the organizers may contribute towards your travel and accommodation costs. There are also many formal associations that organize conferences and training seminars at which speaking engagements are sought.

Before attempting this strategy, you need to be confident in your presentation skills and in your message. You need to have something interesting and captivating to say, and it is essential that you deliver this message well. You are advised to first research the topic in depth, so as to be sure that you can claim to be the expert in it. To test your public speaking skills you may first practise your delivery in the feedback-giving atmosphere of a club concerned with public speaking, or at service clubs such as Rotary. We strongly recommend the section on delivering a talk in Sternberg's (1993) book.

Subsequent to a well-attended presentation, it is not uncommon for some people, to whom your message was particularly relevant, to approach you personally. You will need to have your cards handy to give out. To maximize the effectiveness of your presentation for marketing purposes, ask the other person first for their card or contact details. Once you know who they are, you can follow them up.

5.2.2 *Writing articles and books*

A similar principle applies to that of writing articles or books on the subject of your expertise. Books can add considerably to your reputation, if well done. They will help significantly more if:

- they are produced to proper professional standards by a reputable publisher;
- they are well reviewed in journals or magazines which your potential clients read;
- there is seen to be some practical outcome of your special knowledge.

When these conditions are satisfied, the beneficial publicity is connected to a sometimes undeserved reputation for being a national expert. At the United Nations, they have a saying that 'an expert is someone who has flown over the country at least once; an expert of international repute is someone who has flown over it in daylight'. Notwithstanding these comments, there is no doubt that a good book will enhance your reputation. It will also add to your knowledge and understanding in a way that few other experiences can match.

Books take a considerable time to plan, a long time to write, and an age in production. The long delay in appearing in print also applies to articles in refereed (peer-reviewed) journals. A quicker learning route is to write non-refereed journal articles. Unless your paper is of stunning significance, its appearance in a psychology journal is unlikely to have a beneficial short-term outcome. To this end, you might consider writing for non-psychological forums. If you are in business psychology, writing for business or personnel magazines has much to commend it; if you are in educational psychology, another publication outlet is appropriate.

We have been repeatedly struck by the diffuse effects of reputation: the 'I've heard of you before' statement. Unless the hearing was grossly detrimental, it does convey the impression of being well known and well regarded. In that context, articles that are excellently written and make one or two good points are always in demand. In many cases they will identify you and your practice. Nothing beats having a good article published, for which you are paid as well (being paid to advertise your practice is a benefit that is hard to beat).

5.2.3 Public news media

You do not need to have lots of money to get into the public news media: television, radio and newspapers. To use one of these media to your advantage, you will need to understand how each operates. The information you would like to publicize must be newsworthy, but requirements will be different for different media. For example, to a local paper your practice opening may be a news item. For television, any news item related to your practice has to have a much wider appeal.

If you have become a prominent figure through a public presentation to a seminar or a conference, you may be approached for an interview. You must be prepared and skilled for a live interview to be sure that you will gain rather than lose from the experience. Media appearances can be beneficial if well done, although the risks are considerable. You may find it worthwhile to attend various media workshops offered by trainers. The electronic media in particular go for the 'quick grab'. The brevity of the point and the editing of its presentation carry a serious risk of being misunderstood. Failure to carry a good message to your potential clients may be compounded by a matching disparagement of your competence and probity as determined by your peers.

You do not want to be seen as a Triple-A person (talk on Anything, Anywhere, Anytime). That risk also attaches to being a talkback-show psychologist. If it were that easy, why would serious professionals spend so long doing what they do, and with moderate success, if it could be done in three minutes without even seeing the person? The medium may convey the wrong message.

Readers will appreciate that training in handling the media may be invaluable. To this end the British Psychological Society has published a guide by White *et al.* (1993). Additionally, the British Psychological Society runs a media-training course, details of which are available in a free pamphlet entitled *Media Training*. Furthermore, if there is any prospect of media contact we must strongly urge you to read and remember the BPS Code of Ethics, pages 1 to 2 (Section 1 [General] and Section 2 [Competence] are of good general relevance here). One should also be aware of such issues as preserving confidentiality, making statements only within one's special competence, and of preserving the reputation and dignity of all concerned.

5.2.4 *Voluntary work*

Another strategy of raising one's profile is to do some worthy professional work for no fee. Your local school, your local municipality, or some worthy service club could well use your talents. The amount of unpaid work done in Britain out of generosity of spirit would, if paid, add considerably to the national debt. Doing such work is a way of paying something back to society for the benefits that we enjoy, and fills the heart even if it does not fill the pocket. One cannot predict the business benefits that might flow from such charitable work, but at worst one will have done something constructive and worthwhile, as well as improved a personal reputation.

5.2.5 *Client newsletters*

After your personal marketing effort of visiting your organizational clients and the referrers of your individual clients, you can continually remind them of your existence. One way to do so is always to respond to a referral by writing a 'thank you' letter, and continuing to keep in touch with the referrer. This can only take place if you have received a referral, and you must also remind those who have not referred anyone that your services and your practice still exist.

A useful way of achieving this is through a regular – for example, quarterly or monthly – client newsletter. You would need to ensure that articles are well researched and written in a journalistic style to maximize their readability. If the expense of such a newsletter is prohibitive, your professional association or a more informal network may be able to organize a collective project.

A special format of a newsletter could be a cassette tape, on which you can record a useful but short message about a particular topic that will be of relevance to the receiver. For example, it could be a few stress management tips or a personal development series.

5.2.6 Relationship marketing

As your newsletter or any other communication reaches your client, there is often a positive response: 'Oh, yes. I've been meaning to call you.' This becomes particularly obvious when you follow up your potential client or project referrers personally by telephone. The discussion then develops around the area of need they had. As you do so, you may wonder what would have happened had you not called. The answer is probably, in most cases, nothing: unless the need is pressing, most people tend to spend time on their urgent activities, and your services do not fall into this category.

As you follow up your potential sources of work on a regular basis, the relationships will inevitably develop, even if they are telephone-based. Many successful salespeople refer to their concept of selling as 'relationship-based'. They learn so much about their customers that they can anticipate their needs. Selling a service or product to clients becomes much easier if you understand in what way your offering will benefit them.

To fully gain from this approach, you will first need to keep records on the various pieces of information you have collected about them in your many conversations over the years. Second, and more importantly, you must be genuinely interested in them, and approach this professional relationship in such a way that their needs will become more important to you. Otherwise, your relationship based on intention to sell will be very short-lived, or at least very unproductive.

5.2.7 Developing tangible psychology products

One of the problems of marketing psychology is that its services are not tangible and not easily understood by our society in general. To influence you, the reader, in this area, this handbook has been referring in places to psychology 'products'. To be more effective in your marketing strategy for the practice, it helps to make your services as tangible as possible.

You can turn a generic counselling service into a tangible product by focusing on one aspect, giving it a specific name, calling it a programme, and producing a brochure about it. You can further add to its tangibility by producing a series of cassette tapes or manuals to explain how the counselling is to be used. This process is known as 'branding', namely providing a recognisable brand name for your product.

You can even make a general counselling session tangible by providing the individual client with a report on your diagnosis, including a chart of their test results and a proposed course of intervention. By the client walking out of your practice with a piece of paper, you already have added tangibility to your service. The use of biofeedback in therapy, for example, performs that additional function.

5.2.8 Direct mail

When your services become products, you can more effectively market them through direct mail. It is important to identify clearly your target market before attempting a direct mailing campaign. There are many catalogues of lists of names that can guide you in finding the right group.

Marketing professionals have worked out that the most consistent results come from the classic three-piece mailing, consisting of a letter, a brochure and a response card. Personalized letters tend to do better than those addressed to 'The manager', 'The householder' or some other impersonal form. A letter with a postscript urging the receiver to respond tends to outsell one without. Typing the receiver's address on the response card brings better results than labels, and heavy, quality stock envelopes outperform lighter and cheaper ones. Above all, you first have to ensure that you are sending information to a potential client who is interested in this information and needs the product you are selling.

5.2.9 Telemarketing

One of the best ways to increase the results from your direct mail is to engage telemarketing service providers. They follow up the recipients of your direct mail information and usually make appointments for you to see them. If your product is easily understood and tangible, telemarketing representatives could even finalize sales – to a training seminar, for example, or for receipt of a cassette-tape series.

This sort of marketing is mostly applicable for programmes or products that you can more easily sell on the phone, although your personal visits that will be organized by your telemarketers can also achieve a further result if the telephone call did not do so directly.

5.2.10 *Advertising*

Your services can be advertised in newspapers, electronic media or relevant directories. The rules on advertising apply equally to expanding the practice as to starting it (see Chapter 3). Review the statements of the British Psychological Society code of professional conduct in relation to public announcements and advertising, and comply with them. These are set out on page 16 of the British Psychological Society's *Code of Conduct, Ethical Principles & Guidelines* in the section entitled 'Guidelines on Advertising the Services Offered by Psychologists'.

Apart from announcing your practice generally to the public, advertising works well when you have a specific product – the more tangible the better. It serves either to increase the profile of your practice or to promote a specific programme or service.

5.2.1 *An Internet website*

As explained earlier in section 4.7.7, a more innovative way to introduce your services is by a website on the Internet. While it is relatively inexpensive at the moment, its target market is somewhat undefined, but it clearly includes computer-literate individuals. If your services lend themselves to this sort of advertising, you may consider having a website professionally developed, which will increase its readability. And it is possible to place a counter on it to check the number of visits. When devising a business website, you need to bear in mind that its appearance in one of the best-known search engines (Yahoo!, AltaVista, Searchmsn, etc.) is important.

The use of successful Internet marketing depends, amongst other things, upon having a well-designed home page. That page needs to be clear, user-friendly, and readily accessible. In a competitive environment, your home page needs to rival some very good competitors. The cost of developing a home page may never be recovered if it is not done well and does not produce results.

5.3 Tenders and contracts

Another source of potential work is found in tenders called by corporate and government organizations as well as by business. Tenders are essentially requests for competitive quotations for specifically defined projects or services, such as employee counselling or training needs analyses. 'Closed' tenders are those where the requesting organization pre-selects a number of competing service providers and writes to them directly, seeking their submissions in the form of an Expression of Interest or a Specific Proposal. 'Open' tenders are usually advertised widely through all kinds of media outlets and anyone can apply to provide the required services.

However, scanning for open tenders can be tedious. Those seriously interested in tendering might consider subscribing to a tendering service provider. Such organizations, while they charge a fee, focus on the appropriate tenders for their clients, which can be a significant time-saver.

Applications to fulfil tenders need not be confined to the United Kingdom. Practitioners might consider browsing the website given in Appendix B. There does not seem to be a conventional search engine – but it is a useful site. Access to tender information is provided easily and freely in several countries, but that easy access has some way to go in the United Kingdom. (Now that's an interesting niche market for an enterprising entrepreneur!)

Two particular aspects of tendering are set out next: how to go about applying to tender, and how to maximize the likelihood of success.

5.3.1 How to apply for tender contracts

In preparation for receiving tenders, it is normally accepted that a requesting organization prepares what is called a Consultants' Brief, which outlines the requirements for a tender to do the specified work. You should always obtain this document and any relevant information before submitting your response.

If the Consultants' Brief calls for Expressions of Interest, it is a preliminary call for your credentials and experience in the relevant field. This Expression of Interest is usually a precursor to a call for Proposals. If you are submitting a Proposal, it will normally need to include your approach and a quote in addition to your credentials. Expressions of Interest are equivalent to Capability Statements, which at times are called for by various organizations to select Consultants for their future projects. Such databases of Consultants allow the requesting organizations to put together a shortlist of Consultants and call a closed tender for a particular service or project.

If your Proposal submission is successful, you will usually be invited to attend an interview and, if you are selected to provide the required service, you are very likely to be required to sign a contract for the provision of those services. Whereas it may seem to be a rather bureaucratic process designed for the large organization, it has some advantages for the service provider for it enables a clear definition of the expectations and methods of payment for services provided. You will need to make sure that the contract does not place unreasonable demands on your practice and that you comply with all its clauses. It is always prudent to read such contracts carefully and to ask a solicitor for a professional opinion so that you clearly understand your contractual obligations.

5.3.2 *How to maximize the probability of success*

The process of applying for project work via a tender can be time-consuming and akin to writing a job application. You must keep in mind that you will probably be competing against a large number of other applicants. You cannot expect to win each one of them, but you can do quite a lot to increase your chances of winning.

Some of the hints to maximize your probability of success are:

- Always obtain the Consultants' Brief and get in touch with the organization's representative to check whether there is any other relevant information.
- Keep to the Brief as much as possible in your submission.
- Provide the most relevant experience to the requested project.
- Quote competitively but within your budget to be sure it is actually worthwhile to do the work for your practice.
- Find out all you can about the calling organization, because a tender that shows such insight can give your response that extra edge.

6

Selling your practice

The thought of selling your practice may not be high on your agenda at the time of setting it up. To be sure that your ends will be met by your means, however, this notion may well provide a useful base from which to decide the structure, size and mode of operation of your practice. Your envisioning of what you want your practice to be will enhance the process of your planning.

Sometimes, practitioners reach almost by chance the point of thinking about selling their practice. They have developed their practice slowly over the years and built up a reputation in the marketplace, as well as a corresponding flow of clients, referrals or project work. As they grow tired and wish to take a longer break, or retire from the private-practice lifestyle, they are faced with few options. They can either shut their doors, give it to someone else to manage, or sell it.

Some practitioners may be satisfied to operate a practice that will cease at the point of their retirement or a change in their career direction – in other words, a transient practice, with its beginning and end determined by their own desire to provide their services in the open market and then withdraw them. Any practice that is inextricably linked to the practitioner's individual identity cannot be sold. An alternative view, which you may form, is that you would like your practice to transcend your own identity so that it can outlive your personal presence in the market. This sort of thinking will give rise to a vision that will govern the way you approach the building of your practice.

Whichever outlook applies, some serious thought needs to be given to the process of withdrawal from the practice. Several aspects are discussed in outline in the rest of this chapter.

6.1 Valuing your practice

As soon as the idea of selling a practice is considered, the immediate question on everyone's mind is 'How much is it worth?' In order to find out the answer, the practitioner usually asks the accountant who has been helpful in filling out the taxation-return forms and advising on other business matters. To the practitioner's surprise, it is likely that the accountant does not really know the answer either, because he or she knows little about the details of how a psychology practice really works as a business. There are specialist accountants, however, who tackle such questions with the same professional skill as they would any other business. This is where your practice management, particularly in the financial area, will come under unprecedented scrutiny. There are also agents who specialize in the selling of businesses. It would be worthwhile to consult them.

Whoever buys a business is essentially buying the right to its future cash flow, so the accountants will look to the future for your practice's ability to produce profits and cash. The only way they can do so relatively accurately is by looking at the past, and then asking some probing questions to ascertain whether the past experience can be replicated in the future. The factors that may militate against such replication of past experience will be identified at this stage and costed into the equation.

The most immediate indicator that is used by business valuers is the profits. These are directly related to sales and expenses. The simplest rule of thumb to estimate the value of the business is to multiply the expected net profit by a factor of five. The concept behind such a valuation is that it is reasonable to expect a 20 per cent per annum return on one's investment; hence five time the profits should provide this return. To gauge net profit reasonably accurately for this calculation, it can be obtained from the past records of about three to five years. If the sales have been unusually low or high during this period, the variations need to be explained and possibly averaged.

If you are currently running a practice, it may be worthwhile for you to pause at this stage and consider your profitability, because it is one of the fundamental aspects of the business that will determine the worth of your practice. Even if your profits are hidden in the form of a salary paid to yourself and other directors, there must be a way of proving that your practice is profitable. Otherwise it will be of no other monetary worth than as a not-for-profit charitable organization. (Not that there is anything philosophically wrong with such organizations; quite the opposite, for they are the backbone of our community and societal values.) You just need to ensure that this is what you wanted your practice to become, rather than discovering it by accident, at the end of your private practice career.

The external factors by which the worth of a practice is adjusted revolve around the probability that the business will continue despite the owner leaving the practice. The following issues may be explored as part of this valuation process:

- Is there an established flow of clients?
- Is there some guarantee for the ongoing flow of work?
- Is the range of clients adequately broad?
- Is there an established range of products?
- Will there be a continued demand for services offered?
- Are contracts for services secure or likely to be cancelled?
- Are there any direct competitors?
- Are the premises securely leased?
- To what extent is the practice dependent upon the leaving practitioner's personal qualities, reputation and contacts?

In relation to the last question, if you can demonstrate that the risk of the loss of clients or contracts will be minimal when you depart from the scene, the value of your practice will increase.

6.2 Maximizing the value of your practice

Because psychology practices usually do not have stock, plant or equipment, their value is almost predominantly in their goodwill. Goodwill is not a tangible asset; it can vary widely depending on the factors explored above. A common misconception is that a business 'can always be sold' at some time in the future. This may not necessarily be so, and the worth of your practice will depend to a great extent on the level of your personal involvement in it.

The more your practice is linked to your personal exertion, the less it is worth because the risk of losing clients is greater when you yourself leave. Therefore, the best way to maximize the value of its goodwill is to minimize its dependence on your personal input. One way to do this is to ensure that, if you are dealing with large organizations, there are written and signed contracts in place. Such contracts should not be dependent on your presence in the business. You can also begin to deliberately involve other psychologists in your practice so that the referrers of clients will learn not to depend on you personally being involved in the delivery of professional services.

At the same time, your role should change to ensure that the quality of service does not in any way decrease with your reduced personal involvement. Your practice's worth will therefore depend almost entirely on your business management style. As you invest more time in setting up systems, it will become easier for the practice to function effectively and profitably without you.

6.3 Some implications of the sale

The actual process of selling a practice is something one normally does only once in a lifetime. There are a number of issues that will become obvious as you contemplate this move.

One such issue relates to the matter of privacy and confidentiality. How does one advertise that the practice is for sale without actually diminishing its value by this very advertising? It is important to locate a buyer without alerting the referrers of your clients, so that you can avoid their feeling anxious about the stability of your practice. Likewise, it is best not to alert your competitors to the fact that your practice is for sale, in order to minimize the impact on your market share.

At the same time, it is one of the potential competitors who will be the most likely candidate as a buyer, although a newcomer into the market may choose to purchase an existing practice instead of starting a new one. One way or another you need to locate all potential buyers. You can do this by placing an advertisement in the relevant professional newsletters, bulletins or newspapers. As you do so, it is best to keep the details of the practice confidential and describe it in general terms. Such a description should be adequate to attract an interested party, so you should include estimated financial turnover, geographical area, and the professional area of endeavour. It is also worthwhile requesting assistance from a business trading agent so that the initial filtering of interested parties can take place without disclosing your identity.

6.4 Seeking professional advice on a sale

There are business advisers specializing in valuing and selling professional practices, and the first stop for assistance will be your accountant. Your accountant will need to liaise with your agent closely to enable them to arrive together at the most accurate valuation. It will be most worthwhile to seek such professional assistance well before considering the sale of your practice, so that you may have enough time to establish its real worth and maximize the sale potential. A governmental small-business advice centre (see Appendix B) and any other qualified business adviser can provide valuable assistance in this area.

By this stage of your practice you will have probably learnt that it is important to be aware of your limitations in knowledge and skill and to close the gap by learning from others. As a practitioner and business owner, you will have succeeded in managing your resources so well that the practice continues to thrive after you have departed.

Good luck!

Appendix A: Alternative areas of practice

PRACTICE TYPE	MARKET POPULATION	REFERRER SOURCES
Organizational	Employees Managers/Supervisors Job seekers Entire organizations Teams/Departments	Executive directors Management Training managers Human resource managers

Counselling/Clinical	General public
	Families
	Compensation claimants
	Crime victims
	Employees
		Self
		Medical practitioners
		Community health
		  centres
		Rehabilitation
		  providers
		Insurance agents
		Human resource
		  managers
		Management
		Employee assistance
		managers
		Courts
		Solicitors

Forensic	Compensation claimants Offenders Plaintiffs Defendants	Solicitors Courts Compensation agents
Educational/ Developmental	Students Potential students	Schools Parents Self Community health centres
Vocational/ Occupational	Students Compensation claimants Outplaced employees	Schools Tertiary institutions Rehabilitation providers
Sport	Athletes	Sport clubs Sport associations Self Sports-club coaches

Appendix B: Useful addresses

Note: Due to their constantly changing nature, telephone numbers are not supplied below. Readers may wish to consult the following website for assistance. www.ukphonebook.com

Accountancy

Association of Chartered Certified Accountants, 29 Lincoln's Inn Fields, London WC2A 3EE. **www.acca.co.uk**

Institute of Chartered Accountants in England and Wales, Chartered Accountants Hall, PO Box 433, Moorgate Place, London EC2P 2BJ. **www.icaew.co.uk**

Advertising

The Information Centre of the Advertising Association, Abford House, 15 Wilton Road, London SW1V 1NJ. **www.adassoc.org.uk**

Institute of Practitioners of Advertising, 44 Belgrave Square, London SW1X 8QS. **www.ipa.co.uk**

Business advice

The major banks have excellent starter kits for new businesses. They include useful advice, crucial information, and some contain a diskette with a business plan and other financial programs. Get three such kits and compare.

Business Link. National helpline 0845 7567765. **www.businesslink.co.uk**

European Information Centre. **www.euro-info.org.uk**

Institute of Business Advisers, PO Box 8, Harrogate HG2 8XB. **www.iba.org.uk**

Prime: an initiative for mature enterprise, Walkden House, 3–10 Melton Street, London NW1 2EJ.

The Prince's Youth Business Trust, 18 Park Square East, London NW1 4LH. **www.princes-trust.org.uk**

Shell LiveWire outreach programmes (advice and guidance) contactable on 0845 757 3252. **www.shell-livewire.org.uk**

Technology Means Business, Institute of Management, Cottingham Road, Corby, Northants NN17 1TT. **www.technologymeansbusiness.org.uk**

Governmental bodies

Companies Registration Office, Companies House, Crown Way, Cardiff CF4 3UZ. **www.companieshouse.co.uk**

Department of Trade and Industry, 1 Victoria Street, London SW1H OET. **www.dti.gov.uk**

Inland Revenue – contact your local office

Office of National Statistics. **www.statistics.gov.uk**

Health

National Health Service. National Health Information Service. Freephone 0800 66 55 44, or write to Freepost, LV 6535, Liverpool L2 3BR

Insurance

For professional indemnity insurance, contact Smithson Mason Ltd, SMG House, 31 Clarendon Road, Leeds LS2 9PA. Tel (0113) 294 4000 (ask for BPS unit).

Try also your local insurance brokers for competitive quotes on coverage and premiums. They are listed in the *Yellow Pages* under insurance agents, insurance brokers, and insurance consultants.

Law

Criminal Injuries Compensation Authority, Tay House, 300 Bath Street, Glasgow G2 4JR. **www.cica.gov.uk**

Data Protection Registrar, Wycliff House, Water Lane, Wilmslow, Cheshire SK9 5AF. **www.dataprotection.gov.uk**

Law Society, 113 Chancery Lane, London WC2A IPL.**www.lawsociety.org.uk**

Legal Aid Head Office, Secretariat, 85 Gray's Inn Road, London WC1X 8AA. (There are offices in 14 UK cities; check your local telephone book.) **www.legalservices.gov.uk**

Marketing

Chartered Institute of Marketing, Moor Hall, Cookham, Maidenhead, Berkshire SL6 9QH. **www.cim.org.uk**

Market Research Society, 15 Northburgh Street, London EC1V OJR. **www.mrs.org.uk**

National bodies

British Chambers of Commerce, Manning House, 22 Carlisle Place, London SW1P 1JA. **www.britishchambers.org.uk**

Business Names Registration plc, Somerset House, Temple Street, Birmingham B2 5DN. **www.bnr.plc.uk**

Forum of Private Business, Ruskin Chambers, Drury Lane, Knutsford, Cheshire WA16 6HA. **www.fbp.co.uk**

National Federation of Small Businesses, 32 Orchard Road, Lytham St. Annes, Lancashire FY8 1NY. **www.fsb.org.uk**

The Small Business Bureau Limited, Curzon House, Church Road, Windlesham, Surrey GU20 6BH. **www.smallbusinessbureau.org.uk**

Psychology

The British Psychological Society, St Andrews House, 48 Princess Road East, Leicester LE1 7DR. **www.bps.org.uk**

European Federation of Professional Psychologists Associations, Grasmarkt 105/18, B-1000, Brussels. **www.efppa.org**

Psychotherapy

Psychotherapy Centre (The), 67 Upper Berkeley Street, London W1H 7QX.

UK Council for Psychotherapy, 167–169 Portland Place, London WN1 5FB. **www.psychotherapy.org.uk**

Regional bodies

Highlands & Islands Enterprise, Bridge House, 20 Bridge Street, Inverness IV1 1QR. **www.hie.co.uk**

LEDU, The Small Business Agency for Northern Ireland, LEDU House, Upper Galwally, Belfast BT8 6TB. **www.ledu-ni.gov.uk**

Scottish Enterprise National, 120 Bothwell Street, Glasgow G2 7JP. **www.scottish-enterprise.com**

Welsh Development Agency, Principality House, The Friary, Cardiff CF10 3FE. **www.wda.co.uk**

Tenders

The following sources of information are to be found on the website of the European Commission:

www.europa.eu.int/comm/scr/tender/index_en.htm

www.ted.eur-op.eu.int/ojs/html/index2.htm

See also the CD-ROMs available in your local library: they are likely to contain a supplement to the Official Journal of the European Communities, EUR-OP, which is the official publication of all of the organs of the European Union.

Appendix C: Initial practice capital items: a sample list

BUSINESS FORMATION [1]	
Business Registration	**Company/Trust formation**

FURNITURE[2]	
Professional Office/Room[3]:	Reception/Waiting Room:
1 desk	3 armchairs
1 desk chair	1 coffee table
1 filing cabinet	3 prints/paintings
2 chairs	1 counter/desk
1 cupboard	coffee machine
1 bookshelf	book/information
1 print/painting	library
plants	plants
General Office:	Kitchen:
2 desks	refrigerator
2 typist chairs	1 table
	4 chairs
2 filing cabinets	miscellaneous

EQUIPMENT[4]	
telephone system	photocopier
dictaphone	facsimile machine
computer equipment	video recorder
computer software	tape recorder
printer	security alarm system
biofeedback machine	

STATIONERY	
files/paper/materials	small equipment (staplers etc)

TESTS AND MATERIALS	
selected psychological tests	tapes
books/pamphlets	

SERVICES	
accounting/ business advice	interior decorator
legal advice	computer advice and set-up

PRINTING	
design and layout[5]	compliment slips
letterheads	envelopes
business cards	marketing brochures

MARKETING/ ADVERTISING	
newspaper advertisements	*Yellow Pages* or equivalent
direct mail campaign	

NOTES:

(1) Costs will vary, depending on the business structure you have selected.

(2) All expenditure relating to furniture will not be relevant when you choose to rent premises on a sessional basis or any lease offices that are already furnished.

(3) These figures will have to be multiplied by the number of professional rooms/offices required by the practice.

(4) Some office equipment may be included in the rental of premises, e.g., telephone, security systems and photocopier. Some equipment will be optional, depending on your practice needs – for example a biofeedback machine. If the offices are fully serviced, your needs for word processing may also be provided.

(5) The cost of design is likely to vary greatly depending on the quality of your stationery, the creative skills of your designer and your ability to make quick decisions about the designs you like.

Appendix D: Sample fee schedule

Service description	Service time in hours							
	1/4	1/2	3/4	1	1 1/4	1 1/2	1 3/4	2
Initial consultation	35%	75%	85%	100%	125%	150%	175%	200%
Subsequent consultation	35%	75%	85%	100%	125%	150%	175%	200%
Psychological assessment	35%	75%	85%	100%	125%	150%	175%	200%
Psychological testing session	40%	80%	95%	105%	130%	155%	180%	205%
Neuropsychological assessment	35%	75%	85%	100%	125%	150%	175%	200%
Report preparation	Allow requisite number of hours, depending on length and complexity							
Case conference	Charge as per standard consultation rates (minimum 15 minutes)							
Telephone consultation	Charge as per standard consultation rates (minimum 15 minutes)							
Travel time	Charge as per standard consultation rates, no charge for travel expenses							
Group consult (2-9 clients)		80%	100%	120%	140%	160%	180%	
Family group (2-4 clients)		80%	100%	120%	140%	160%	180%	
Family group (3-9 clients)		90%	110%	130%	150%	170%	190%	
Attendance at court	Attendance fee by negotiation							
Waiting time at court	After agreed time charge at standard rate							

Notes
1   It is assumed that clients will not be charged for extras, such as test materials, etc.
2   Where sessions are in excess of two hours negotiate a special fee.
3   Have a clear policy about charges for missed appointments.
4   Consider percentage inducements for prompt payment.

References

Barclays Bank (1999). Business Bulletin (Issue 2 of 1999). *Small Businesses Surviving Longer.*

Bartram D. (ed.) (1997). *Review of Ability and Aptitude Tests (Level A): for Use in Occupational Settings.* Leicester: BPS Books.

Bartram D. and Lindley P. A. (2000). *Psychological Testing: the BPS 'Level A' Open Learning Programme* (revised and updated edition). Leicester: BPS Books.

Blanchard, K. and Johnson, S. (1982). *The One Minute Manager.* London: Fontana/Collins.

Block, P. (1981). *Flawless Consulting.* San Diego: Pfeiffer & Company.

British Psychological Society (1995). *Professional Practice Guidelines.* (Division of Clinical Psychology.)

British Psychogical Society (1995). *Professional Psychology Handbook.* Leicester: BPS Books.

British Psychological Society (1995). *Psychological Testing: A User's Guide.* (Steering Committee on Test Standards.)

British Psychological Society (1996). *Private Practice as a Psychologist.* November.

British Psychological Society (1998). *Criteria for Membership.* November.

British Psychological Society (1999). *Careers in Psychology.* February.

British Psychological Society (1999). *Chartered Psychologists.* December.

British Psychological Society (1999). *Conversion Qualifications.* September.

British Psychological Society (1999). *Guidance on the Complaints, Investigatory and Disciplinary Procedures.*

British Psychological Society (1999). *Information on the Register of Chartered Psychologists.* November.

British Psychological Society (1999). *Information on the Sections and Special Groups of the Society.*

British Psychological Society (1999). *Guidelines for the Development and Use of Computer Based Assessments.* May.

British Psychological Society (1999). *How to Reach Psychologists'.* November.

British Psychological Society (1999). Memo on *'Use of the Society Logo'.* 24 May.

British Psychological Society (1999). *Non-evaluative UK Test Publishers.* (Steering Committee on Test Standards.)

British Psychological Society (1999). *Steering Committee on Test Standards: Non-Evaluative UK Test Publishers List.* July.

British Psychological Society (2000). *Information on the Divisions of the Society.*

British Psychological Society (2000). *Code of Conduct, Ethical Principles and Guidelines.*

British Psychological Society (2000). *Media Training.*

British Psychological Society (2001). *Responsibility and accountability in clinical psychology.* (Division of Clinical Psychology.)

British Psychological Society (periodically updated). *The Directory of Chartered Psychologists.*

British Psychological Society (periodically updated). *The Register of Chartered Psychologists.*

British Psychological Society (undated). *Certificate and Register of Competence in Occupational Testing.*

British Psychological Society (undated). *Steering Committee on Test Standards. Psychometric Testing.*

British Psychological Society (undated). *Steering Committee on Test Standards: Psychometric Testing (frequently asked questions – and their answers).*

British Psychological Society (undated). *Professional Liability Insurance for Psychologists.*

Covey, S.R. (1993). *The Seven Habits of Highly Effective People – Restoring the Character Ethic.* Melbourne: The Business Library, Information Australia.

Criminal Injuries Compensation Authority (1999). *A Guide to the Criminal Injuries Compensation Scheme* (updated and well indexed).

Criminal Injuries Compensation Scheme (1995). *The Criminal Injuries Compensation Scheme* (the formal statement).

Cronin, A.J. (1952). *Adventure in Two Worlds.* London: Gollancz.

Francis R. D. (1999). *Ethics for Psychologists: A Handbook.* Leicester: BPS Books.

Francis, R.D. and Cameron, C. (1997). *The Professional Psychology Handbook.* Melbourne: Macmillan.

Gale, A. (1990). 'Applying psych to the psych degree: Pass with first class honours, or miserable failure'. *The Psychologist,* 3, 483–8.

Gerber, M. (1995). *The E-myth Revisited – Why Most Small Businesses Don't Work and What to Do about It.* New York: Harper Collins.

Haywood P. (1998). *DIYPR: The Small Business Guide to 'Free' Publicity.* London: Batsford.

Kasperczyk, R. and Francis, R.D. (1997). *The Manual of Private Psychology Practice.* Melbourne: Macmillan.

Kat, B. (1998). 'Use of electronic records as the professional record'. *The Psychologist.* January, 23–6.

Kent, P. (1994). *The Complete Idiot's Guide to the Internet.* (2nd ed.). Indianapolis: Alpha Books, NY: Macmillan Publishing.

Kruithof J. and Ryall, J. (1994). *The Quality Standards Handbook – How to Understand and Implement Quality Systems and ISO 9000 Standards in a Context of Total Quality and Continuous Improvement.* Melbourne: The Business Library, Information Australia.

Kruithof, J. (1993). *Quality Thinking — How to Implement a Quality Philosophy, in your Thinking and Through Personal Change.* Melbourne: The Business Library, Information Australia.

Legal Aid (1999). *A Practical Guide to Legal Aid.*

Legal Aid (1999). *Legal Aid: How to get Free Low-Cost Legal Help.*

Legal Aid (1999). *Criminal Legal Aid at the Police Station and in Court.*

Law Society, The (1999). *Lawyers for your Business: Succeed in Business, the Legal Angle.*

Lindley P. A. (2001). *Review of Personality Assessment Instruments.* (2nd ed.). Leicester: BPS Books.

Mort, D. (Compiler) (1990). *Sources of Unofficial UK Statistics.* Aldershot: Gower.

Nathan, G. (1993). *Managing the Franchisor/Franchisee Relationship.* Parramatta, NSW: Franchisors Association of Australia and New Zealand.

National Health Service (1999). *The Patient's Charter and You.* Department of Health.

NatWest (1999). *Mind Your Business.* (On insurance needs.)

Samson, D. (1988). *Preparing a Business Plan.* Canberra: Australian Government Publishing Service.

Sternberg, R. (1993). *The Psychologist's Companion,* Cambridge: Cambridge University Press.

Wallace, P (1999). *The psychology of the internet.* Cambridge: Cambridge University Press.

White, S., Evans, P., Mihill, C. and Tysoe, M. (1993). *Hitting the Headlines: A Practical Guide to the Media.* Leicester: BPS Books.

Index